Praise for Daniel Friedmann's

The Genesis One Code

"The book is engrossing. His presentation is persuasive and devoid of insistence. In essence, he argues that, just as a blueprint provides a scale reference to the finished building, there is a mathematical scale that reconciles the events of Genesis to the findings of science." — *The National Post*

"How things started has been a hot topic since Darwin's theory of evolution and the subsequent discoveries of physicists and scientists throughout the subsequent centuries. Usually a book appears as a rant, descrying the 'other side' of the debate from the vantage of the writer's opinion. The genuine pleasure of reading this book is the gentle manner in which the author marries the two concepts, not debunking either, but demonstrating through his scholarship how he believes that scientific theory and spiritual theory enhance each other.

What the book does not do is further separate the two visions of the beginning of the universe and the beginning of life: Friedmann has taken the time to study the forms of the various names of the creator and the terms of the steps of development of the universe as we have grown to know it and to explore it, and in doing so he acts as the glue to bind both theories, putting to rest the hostilities of the arguments from both sides as being the only way conceivable!

Whether the reader enters this discussion from the purely religious side or from the purely scientific side, the one (of many) points that Friedmann makes is that there is no reason for combative separatism."

— *Grady Harp, Hall of Fame/TOP 50 Reviewer, Amazon*

"Regardless of where you stand when it comes to the origin of the universe, The Genesis One Code is a worthwhile read. I could not put it down once I was finally able to start reading…and it certainly did provide me with some fresh insight as to how creation from a Catholic standpoint can be in agreement with creation from a scientific standpoint."

— The Catholic Science Geek

"Daniel Friedmann's breakout book, The Genesis One Code, provides the reader with an excellent comparison between biblical teaching and scientific theory. It is a read you don't want to miss. When was the dawn of creation? Six thousand years ago with a divine act or 14 billion years ago with the Big Bang. Friedmann does not try to influence readers one way or the other. The Genesis One Code is masterfully done."

— Richard Sand, award winning author

"Friedmann gives us an opportunity to reconcile divergent views on creation in a thoughtful and insightful work. Will the two sides heed this offer for greater understanding or will they see his work as peripheral and find some superficial "sound bite" way to dismiss him. Time will tell. Regardless, he has done us all a service by taking this high road of reconciliation while maintaining the integrity of the two opposing sides."

— CFO large, high tech company

"I really enjoyed reading The Genesis One Code. Friedmann writes in a pointed voice, easy to understand and follow, supporting his ideas with referenced resources. The Bible dates back so much farther than scientific discovery and it's always bothered me that science attempts to discount that God created the world. It makes me much happier to see an alignment of science and creation, since God created both anyway! Five stars for this book!"

— Planet Weidknecht

"If you are looking to read something that will increase your knowledge as well as make you think about your own viewpoints, this is the book for you. I also recommend this book for Catholics who, although have no "official" teaching on the Evolution and Big Bang Theories, are encouraged to come to their own positions that compliment faith and science. *The Genesis One Code* will provide an insight towards thinking of religion and science as complimentary disciplines that can both lead humanity to understanding the truth."

— Br. Vito Martinez, Capuchin Franciscans

"For those who question how to reconcile the biblical account of the beginnings of the universe with the scientific theory of the Big Bang, Daniel Friedmann's The Genesis One Code will be a welcome read, especially as we witness the origins debate seep into the public's political, social, educational and theological conversations. By placing the two accounts side by side, Friedmann examines the timelines provided in the Book of Genesis and the Big Bang theory, and finds a great deal of overlap." *— Jewish Independent newspaper*

INSPIRED STUDIES

BOOK 1

Second Edition

The Genesis One Code

Daniel Friedmann

Inspired Books

For information: Inspired Books
www.danielfriedmannbooks.com

ISBN: 978-0-9784572-1-1

10 9 8 7 6 5 4 3 2 1

Dedication

To Michael, Zach and Jane, who ask deep questions and are not afraid to explore answers from diverse bodies of knowledge.

Table of Contents

FIGURES

TABLES

Acknowledgements

Many people were instrumental in helping me with this work. My Kabbalah teachers of many years, Rabbi Avraham Feigelstock and Rabbi Shmuel Yeshayahu, introduced me to key concepts and helped me locate references. Eliezer Zieger made time for numerous telephone conversations to discuss key topics and provide help with references.

My effort to ensure that the sometimes abstruse documentation in this work appeared in a form suitable for general readers was aided by the encouragement and assistance of Hugh, Julio, Nora and Suresh. In addition, Debra Christian of The Happy Guy Marketing Inc. provided critical editorial assistance.

I would like also to express my gratitude for the help and advice given me by my wife, Marilyn, who patiently edited, critiqued and formatted the manuscript.

Ron V. May, of Park East Press, carefully edited the manuscript and made numerous excellent suggestions toward an essential contribution to the finished work.

Foreword

Are you educated in the sciences and convinced that current scientific theories and data explain our origins? At the same time, do you have an awareness of the Bible and its seeming incompatibility with science?

Do you believe that God created the world and that all answers pertaining to our origins are clearly provided in the scriptures? At the same time, do you have a basic awareness of science and its seeming incompatibility with some of the teachings of your religion?

Are you familiar with the basics of both religion and science, yet cannot reconcile the two as far as explaining our origins?

At the start of this journey I too was unsure whether or not the answers found in science books and religious scriptures could be reconciled. Now, having explored both in some depth, I can say that such reconciliation is not out of the question. This book attempts to demonstrate the reconciliation with respect to two major areas: the timing of the formation of the universe, and the emergence and development of life on earth. First, let me tell you about my background and potential biases.

I began with knowledge gained from a basic religious upbringing and a high school science education. Both bodies of knowledge were fascinating, yet appeared incompatible. As I proceeded to obtain a scientific education, I initially came to think that science books answered everything. Yet, by my fourth year at university, some fundamental questions concerning our origins began to reappear. In science texts, some answers were not available, some answers were strange, and some answers were so metaphysical they looked like religious answers. So, I went back to study religion, this time also studying the mystical component of religion so as to find deeper inner meaning rather than the simple interpretation. Answers to my questions began to appear.

The Genesis creation narrative, for Christians and Jews, provides the fundament for an understanding of their origins. For Muslims, too, it is an important component of the same understanding. While *The Genesis One Code* is based primarily on the creation narrative, in order to delve deep into the subject's mysteries I relied on Jewish sources exclusively, since Judaism has formed the background of my religious education. Of those with different religious backgrounds or none at all, I would ask that you please continue to read on. You may find that the various sources pertaining to origins have more in common than perhaps expected. Certainly, such widely divergent narratives as the six days of creation as revealed in religious texts versus the billions of years as described in scientific theories present a key challenge for us all. They would seem incompatible, irreconcilable. I maintain they are not.

This book presents a direct and rigorous analysis of creation events and their times of occurrence as described in both Genesis and in the latest scientific books and papers. No attempt is made to either discredit or excuse any body of knowledge or any person's particular religious belief. On the contrary, the thesis of *The Genesis One Code* is that both science texts and the Bible effectively describe our universe and its development.

No attempt is made herein to present why they are either compatible or incompatible by providing arguments that, although potentially powerful, cannot be proved conclusively. Instead, in *The Genesis One Code* every attempt is made to reconcile religion-based creation events and their timing with the same events as studied by scientists. When we put aside our personal beliefs and focus only on the events and their timing, we find an alignment—a startling alignment. This book aims to elucidate the alignment. My wish is that once you have glimpsed such alignment, you then can ponder our origins with a newly reconciled set of stories—the biblical story, which is thousands of years old, and the scientific story, which is very new.

Chapter 1

Introduction

Imagine there exist medieval manuscripts, written some 800 years ago, that could help us decipher Genesis and thereby pinpoint exactly when the universe began—an instant squaring, moreover, with our most up-to-date cosmological theories.

Further, suppose these same manuscripts could help us extract from Genesis unequivocal timelines for the development of life on earth, again precisely as identified by the latest scientific evidence derived from the fossil record. We are not talking about roughly similar timelines. We are talking about exactly the same timelines.

Currently, evidence obtained and compiled through use of the scientific method has shown the universe to be 13.7 billion years old. Similar scientific work has shown that life emerged on earth some 3.5 billion years ago and is further theorized to have developed by a process of Darwinian natural selection, eventually evolving into the numerous species we have today. Religion, which comprises sets of beliefs concerning the cause, nature, and purpose of the universe and humankind, is based on a personal faith in supernatural causes. For many believers, God created the universe and life in six days, and moreover, at a time less than 6,000 years ago. Scientific and religious timelines would indeed seem incompatible. However, could it be they are simply using different terms to describe the same phenomenon?

So what, then, of these 800-year-old medieval manuscripts? They exist, and one in particular has recently been translated into English and can help us further interpret Genesis, a key component of Judaism and Christianity.

Hard to believe? It is worth reiterating: the rigorous approach of science and a careful and equally rigorous analysis of Genesis produce exactly the same timelines for the formation of the universe and for the development of life on earth.

Currently, the creation-evolution debate has pitched religion against science. But if the goal of this book is achieved, we will come closer to reconciling the two approaches and solve a highly contentious element of the dispute, the disagreement over timelines.

The creation-evolution controversy (or the origins debate) is a recurring cultural, political, and theological dispute (primarily in the United States) about the origins of earth, humanity, life, and the universe. The dispute is between those who espouse religious belief in the supernatural, and thus support a creationist view, versus those who believe natural explanations alone are sufficient to explain origins and thus accept evolution as supported by scientific consensus.

The creation-evolution controversy originated in Europe and North America in the late eighteenth century, when discoveries in geology led to various theories of an ancient earth, and fossils showing past extinctions prompted early ideas of evolution. Religious believers responded to the old earth evidence by interpreting the six days of creation as six epochs. This accommodation of the timelines allowed the dialogue between science and religion to continue into the early twentieth century. However, both sides have become more polarized in their views, and dialogue has decreased significantly during the past half century. Many religious believers have moved toward a fundamentalist interpretation of a literal six days, and scientists to a strict view of evolution as a struggle for survival among randomly mutating genes, with no room for God.

Today the general public[1] remains divided by the origins debate. Surveys indicate that half believe God specially created the first humans. Most of the rest affirm that God guided evolution.

Only about 15% accept the God-less theory of origins that dominates science.

An unresolved component of the debate continues to be the timeline issue: 6,000 years versus 13.7 billion years.

Before we can establish a corresponding timeline between science and religions that are based on the six-day creation belief, we'll briefly describe the basis of knowledge for each area of study. Our scope will be to explain the scientific approach as well as the biblical account of the beginning of existence as we know it. A comparison will explore the seemingly contradictory nature of both accounts and reveal startling parallel developments—albeit during strikingly different time frames among the scientific and biblical perspectives. As shall be seen, these two measurements of time do not contradict each other but actually flow in parallel fashion and are fully synchronized.

Science is the systematic process of gathering information about the world and organizing it into theories and laws that can be tested. To be considered scientific, a body of knowledge must pass certain objective tests. The scientific method is a system of processes used to establish new or revised knowledge. A scientific approach is applied to collecting factual information. To be termed scientific, a method of inquiry must be based on gathering unbiased evidence through observation, experience, and experiment.

Of course, certain reasoning and logic have to be followed when testing theories and hypotheses. Objectivity is a defining approach to studies of this type. Following scientific observation, the results must be organized, summarized, and applied to develop and test theories. Typically, after the process of peer review, findings are shared with an audience of qualified persons in the field of study, as well as possibly the public at large or some portion of it. Scientists scrutinizing a test result or theory may attempt to prove or disprove the original study's findings by reproducing the observation or experimentation under identical conditions; scientists also may perform new tests.

The scientific approach works very well when applied to extant phenomena and events. But what about events that occurred long ago, say 13.7 billion years ago?

Amazingly, scientists today can observe the results of what happened almost back to the estimated date of the universe's origins. Nonetheless, there is no recording, written or otherwise, of what actually jump-started the birth of the universe. The only existing evidence of the universe's formation is derived from what we can perceive through instruments, these detecting primarily instances of light and sound within the physical world surrounding us and on to distant yet still perceivable heavenly bodies. For what stretches past our instrument-aided vision and into unexplored realms beyond—that is to say, what surpasses our ability to see as well as to comprehend—we must rely on conjecture deriving from theories and mathematics.

Further, our physical origins cannot be re-experienced. The beginning happened once before—only once—and it cannot be duplicated in precisely the same way.

Therefore, in the realm of scientific inquiry we are left with experimentation to prove the most reasonable theories of the universe's origins. Accordingly, scientists and researchers continue to conduct tests on multiple hypotheses based on observation of our present geological world and astral space, as well as to process experience gleaned from historical and current events recorded throughout Human Time. Satellite observations, meteor strikes, telescopic studies, and even a moon landing are among the ways scientists are learning more about earth's place in the cosmos.

Still, all the knowledge that continues to be collected regarding the nature of our universe leaves some questions unanswered. Many who study the science believe the theory of a 13.7 billion-year-old universe and a 4.5 billion-year-old earth is relatively accurate, based on findings to date. But for many, this body of information is inadequate, or even inaccurate. For them, God is the architect of creation as revealed through His inspired Word in the Holy Scriptures known as the Bible.

For many Christian and Jewish believers, the Five Books of Moses are considered to be the revealed Word of God. To some, this means the words contained in the Five Books of Moses, along with other scriptures and the oral tradition that elaborates and explains the five books, were given to Moses exactly in the form we have them today. To others, this means that God spoke to men— mainly prophets—who recorded His words in the book widely known as the Bible. Scholars estimate that the Bible was written by 40 people over a span of 2,000 years. Finally, to non-believers the Bible is a collection of ancient myths and fables. The Bible itself has been translated into numerous editions, with the most widely read version likely the 1611 King James Version. Newer and more recent translations are perhaps better understood by many today owing to the use of contemporary language rather than the early modern Elizabethan dialect that seems stilted and inaccessible to twenty-first century readers.

Genesis is the first book of the Bible, and the first of the five books of the Law (the Pentateuch) ascribed by tradition to Moses. Beginning with the creation of the universe and humankind, the narrative relates the initial disobedience of the man and the woman and their consequent expulsion from God's garden. Genesis, which means beginnings, contains the entire creation account; the first chapter of Genesis contains 31 verses describing God's acts of creating the universe and the world within a six-day period. The second chapter of Genesis, comprising 25 verses, elaborates on God's creation of human life in a man He called Adam, and from his side, a woman who was named Eve and became Adam's wife. From this pair of ancestors and their children, we are told, came all human life. The third chapter of Genesis describes the downfall of Adam and Eve as a result of their sin (see Annex A for the full text of the first three chapters of Genesis).

The Genesis account provides a six-day creation period of the universe while revealing a specific order of events: [2]

> *In the beginning God created the heaven and the earth. And the earth was without form, and void; and darkness was upon the face of the deep. And the Spirit of God moved upon the face of the waters. And God said, Let there be light: and there was light. And God saw the light, that it was good: and God divided the light from the darkness. And God called the light Day, and the darkness he called Night. And the evening and the morning were the first day.*

Many adherents of two major world religions—Christianity and Judaism—accept the Genesis account as factual and literal. We will more closely examine the religious implications of the Genesis account in a later chapter. But it should be mentioned that the five books of Moses are not just a collection of religious scriptures. They include an account of creation, some early history of human life, and many laws and commandments.

The relationship between the holy books of these two religions is illustrated below in Figure 1.1, showing that both religions share the five books of Moses and Psalms, in addition to other texts.

The Holy Bible, the sacred writings of the Christian religion, includes the Old Testament (containing 39 books of Hebrew scripture, including the five books of Moses), and the New Testament, which includes the four Gospel accounts of Jesus' life and teachings, as well as letters, mainly from the Apostle Paul, that were written to encourage and inspire new church groups that sprang up in the wake of Jesus' ministry.

Not shown in Figure 1.1 is the Islamic holy book the Qur'an and other revelations, which most Muslims believe were dictated by God to various Islamic prophets. These revelations include the Tawrat (given to Moses and which is close[3] to the five books of Moses), the Zabur (revealed to David and close to Psalms), and the Injil (teachings revealed through Jesus). The account of creation in the Qur'an is similar in some ways to the account in Genesis. However, Islamic teaching on creation differs in critical ways. In particular, although the Qur'an does declare that creation occurred in six days, days are interpreted not as literal twenty-four hour periods but as stages or other periods of time.

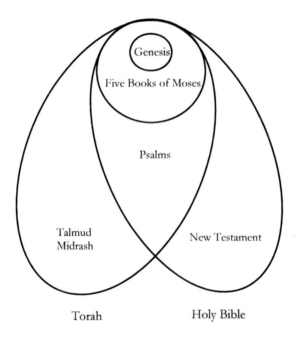

Figure 1.1 Sacred Texts of Christians and Jews

Genesis is one of the five books of spiritual law derived from God, known as the Written Law. For Jews, the Written Law is interpreted and applied with the aid of the Oral Law (now documented in writing). The Oral Law includes the Talmud and the Zohar. The Talmud (meaning instruction, learning) is a central text of mainstream Judaism in the form of a record of rabbinic discussions pertaining to Jewish law, ethics, philosophy, customs, and history. The Zohar (meaning splendor or radiance) is the foundational work in the literature of Jewish mystical thought known as

Kabbalah; it is a group of books, including commentary, addressing the mystical aspects of the five books of Moses and matters of scriptural interpretation, while also including material on the nature of God, the origin and structure of the universe, the nature of souls, and psychology. Together, the Written and Oral Law comprise the Torah.[4]

For believers, the Torah contains legal and ethical instructions. Although not primarily intended to be a science textbook, the Torah, for those who believe it is the revealed word of God, presents an accurate representation of our world. In fact, the Talmudic sages teach that "God looked into the Torah and created the world." [5] The Torah is the blueprint of the universe and for humankind's existence from a faith-based perspective, and is drawn from a tradition of oral and written principles. This religious system of beliefs will be examined more closely later.

Thus, given that the scientific method should produce accurate descriptions of the universe, and accepting that the Torah is the blueprint of the universe, key facts about the universe discussed in the Torah (and in particular Genesis) and that likewise are arrived at by the scientific method must be equal. Indeed, this is the very thesis outlined and developed in detail throughout this book by means of Torah sources and peer-reviewed scientific sources, namely: the answers provided by science and Torah are exactly equal.

How can this be?

The widely accepted Big Bang theory and scientific observation have, in recent years, been synthesized to develop a timeline of major events in the development of the universe over the past 13.7 billion years.[6] The Big Bang theory suggests that the universe was originally very hot and dense, and then about 13.7 billion years ago it began to expand quickly. The universe has since cooled while continuing to expand. This theory is based on observed, scientific evidence.

A proponent of an early version of this theory was Georges Lemaître, a Belgian Roman Catholic priest and physicist, who based his study on Albert Einstein's theory of general relativity. The Big Bang model is not yet able to explain the origins of primal singularity from which the constituents of the universe and the laws of physics emerged. It does, however, powerfully describe the development of the universe from that time period. As time went on, matter created in the original blast continued to expand, which led to the formation of slightly denser areas that, due to gravity, attracted additional matter and became dense enough to form stars, galaxies, and other astronomical bodies.

Continuously improving telescope technology has led to corresponding adjustments and updates to the Big Bang theory. One discovery was the idea that the universe's expansion seems to be increasing in speed.

Although many Christians rejected the idea of a slowly evolving universe that seemed to contradict the model of creation found in Genesis, in 1951 Roman Catholicism, under the leadership of Pope Pius XII, embraced the Big Bang theory and declared it compatible with the creation account found in Genesis.

> It would seem that present-day science, with one sweep back across the centuries, has succeeded in bearing witness to the august instant of the primordial *Fiat Lux* [Let there be Light], when along with matter, there burst forth from nothing a sea of light and radiation, and the elements split and churned and formed into millions of galaxies.[7]

However, the time discrepancy between creation and the Big Bang remained unanswered.

What, then, about life on earth?

Life on earth has left a clear, measurable record. Fossils are the preserved remains or traces of animals, plants, and other organisms from the remote past. The totality of fossils, both discovered and undiscovered, and their placement in fossil-containing rock formations and sedimentary layers (strata) is known as the fossil record. Fossils vary in size from microscopic, such as single bacterial cells only one micrometer in diameter, to gigantic, such as dinosaurs and trees many meters long and weighing several tons. Absolute dating methods have been used to verify the relative ages obtained by fossils and to provide absolute ages for many fossils. The fossil record depicts life's history during its unfolding across 3.5 billion years and has been used to develop a timeline of major events in the development of life on earth.

Integrating the timeline from the Big Bang and the timeline obtained from the fossil record allows us to scientifically and chronologically date key events from the beginning of the universe 13.7 billion years ago until the present day. The first two chapters in the book of Genesis discuss some of the same key events described by the scientific timelines. Genesis sets these events on an initial six-day creation timeline, whereas the biblical calendar then dates subsequent events over a period of less than 6,000 years. These science- and Bible-derived timelines lead to large apparent discrepancies for the timing of events.

To address these discrepancies, a discussion of time is required. Scientists have established that time has a beginning, may have an end, and is different for people within different frames of reference.[8] The Big Bang theory leads to an initial singularity from which the universe and time emerged—the beginning of time. Current theories under development[9] are in dispute; however, some point to many scenarios under which time, and perhaps also the universe, end. Einstein's theories of special relativity and general relativity, although counter-intuitive, show that people moving with respect to each other and/or in dissimilar gravitational fields experience time differently, and neither is absolute or universally correct. These theories have been tested and proved.

Similarly, time in the Bible has a beginning and an end, and is different for the two conscious, separate observers of which the Bible speaks: God and man. Genesis sets out from a point "in the beginning" of time. The scriptures tell us, as will be elaborated later in the book, that the world will attain a messianic age and eventually will perhaps cease to have a physical manifestation. Finally, the scriptures and their mystical interpretation reveal that time is kept differently in the physical world and in the various spiritual strata, or worlds.[10] In this respect, we are told in Psalms that one day for God is equivalent to 1,000 years as experienced by humans.[11]

In both science and the Torah there is the concept of the conscious observer—a being observing and interpreting reality. In science, theory and experiment have revealed that the observer and his or her measurements affect the end result of an experiment in the microscopic quantum world. Recently it has been shown that quantum mechanics applies at all scales[12], although the implications of this discovery are not yet well understood. In the Torah, these ideas definitely apply[13] to our macroscopic world. In Kabbalah, which is a mystical interpretation of the Torah, the conscious observer determines as well as causes reality. People interpret the Torah and make rulings on matters according to the law. These rulings, in turn, influence human physical reality.

We now begin to see how to correlate the biblical timeline with the scientific one. God keeps time differently than people do. There was an earlier period in which God was the conscious observer, and a later period (still ongoing) wherein man and woman are the conscious observers. For the period when God was the conscious observer, we must convert from God's time to the time that a human measures.

This is not a modern concept. Isaac ben Samuel of Acre[14] (fl. 13th-14th century), a Kabbalist who lived in the land of Israel 800 years ago, was the first to state that the universe is actually billions of years old, at a time when the prevalent thought was that the universe was thousands of years old. Isaac arrived at this conclusion by distinguishing between time as experienced by humans and time as experienced by God, herein described as Human Time and Divine Time, respectively. However, his work was only brought to light recently in English by Rabbi Aryeh Kaplan (1979).[15] More recently, this approach to calculating the age of the universe has been expanded in more detail from a physics point of view.[16, 17, 18] These previous attempts at calculating the age of the universe were made in an approximate fashion. They provide estimates for the age of the universe of over 15 billion years, which are clearly too high to match current scientific data. These approximate methods also prevent an accurate estimation of other events, such as how long animals have inhabited the earth.

This work attempts to perform a more accurate formulation of time when God was the conscious observer. The focus will provide for the calculation of the precise age of the universe and makes possible the comparison of key biblical events to scientifically derived dates for these same events. This comparison can be made to better than 100 million years, which is ten times more accurate than previous time frame estimates, in the range of a few billion years.

This book is organized in the following structure:

In Chapter 2, the history of the controversy between science and religion is summarized, with emphasis on the role of the timeline discrepancy. We see a division between science and religion that can perhaps begin to be reconciled if their vastly different timelines can be matched.

In Chapter 3, the Big Bang and the fossil record are described, including exactly what they reveal and where questions remain. This information serves as reference background on the current state of scientific knowledge regarding the development of the universe and appearance of life on earth, and which is used for comparison with similar information described in the creation narrative in subsequent chapters.

In Chapter 4, the key Torah sources and authors used toward developing the interpretation of Genesis are briefly outlined. This information provides background on the biblical references used in subsequent chapters.

In Chapter 5, the conversion of timelines is provided:

—The creation timeline is described and drawn to the best accuracy known, using hours, not days.

—Divine Time, or time as measured by God, is plotted on a parallel timeline showing its conversion to the creation timeline.

—Human Time, or time as measured by a human being, is additionally plotted in parallel, demonstrating its conversion to Divine Time.

A method to convert Creation Time to time as measured by science having been established, biblical Creation Time is then compared with scientifically derived time for key events:

In Chapter 6, the age of the universe is computed from the creation narrative and compared to the scientific estimate.

In Chapter 7, all cosmological events described in the creation narrative are compared alongside the events predicted by the Big Bang theory.

In Chapter 8, the sequence and timing of the appearance of life on earth as described in the creation narrative are compared alongside the fossil record.

In Chapter 9, the times of the major extinctions of life are derived from events in the creation narrative and compared alongside the times for the extinctions of life observed in the fossil record.

Chapter 10 discusses the timeline for the development of humankind.

By the time we reach Chapter 11, the book's conclusion, it will be clear that Human Time and Creation Time are harnessed in tandem. Understanding the correlation between the two time frames, and therefore between events in the past, brings us to a new level of understanding and questioning of our origins.

---

[1]   Edward J. Larson, *The Theory of Evolution: A History of Controversy* (U.S.A. The Teaching Company, 2002), p. 34.

[2]   Genesis 1:1-5, The Holy Bible, King James Version. New York: Oxford Edition: 1769; King James Bible Online, 2008. http://www.kingjamesbibleonline.org/.

[3]   Many Muslims believe the Judeo-Christian scriptures have been corrupted and are therefore inaccurate views of the actual revelations to Moses, David, and Christ.

[4]   The Torah comprises Written Law: Five Books of Moses, Prophets, Writings (i.e., Psalms), Sanhedrin, Rabbinical Laws and Customs; and Oral Law: Talmud (Mishna, Gemarah), Explanations, Midrashim, Zohar. All biblical quotes and commentaries (unless otherwise referenced) are from translations found in *The Stone Edition Chumash, the Torah, Haftaros, and Five Megillos, with a Commentary from Rabbinic Writings*, General Editors Rabbi Nosson Scherman and Rabbi Meir Zlotowitz (New York: Mesorah Publications Ltd., 2009). All Talmud quotes are from the English translations found in *Soncino Babylonian Talmud*, Ed. Rabbi Dr. I. Epstein (London: The Soncino Press, 1935-1948).

[5]   Midrash Rabbah on Genesis 1:2; Zohar I:134a, Vol. II, 161b.

[6]   Mark Whittle, *Cosmology: The History and Nature of Our Universe, Course Guidebook* (U.S.A.: The Teaching Company, 2008).

[7]   Martin Gorst, *Measuring Eternity* (Broadway Books, 2001), pp. 254-255.

[8]   George Musser, "Could Time End?" *Scientific American* 303 (3), September 2010, pp. 84-91.

[9]   Ibid.

[10]   Eliezer Zeiger, "Time, Space and Consciousness." BOr HaTorah Vol. 15, ed. Prof. Herman Branover (Israel: SHAMIR, 2005).

[11]   "For a thousand years in your sight are but like yesterday when it is past" (Psalm 90:4) as interpreted in the Babylonian Talmud, Sanhedrin 97a and 97b.

[12]   Vlatko Vedral, "Living in a Quantum World," *Scientific American*, June 2011, pp. 38-43.

[13]   Avi Rabinowitz and Herman Branover, "The Role of the Observer in Halakhah and Quantum Physics," eds. H. Branover and I. Attia, (Northvale, NJ: *Science in the Light of the Torah: A B'or HaTorah Reader*, 1994).

[14]   Kaufmann Kohler, M. Seligsohn, Isaac ben Samuel of Acre, 2002, JewishEncyclopedia.com.

[15]   Rabbi Aryeh Kaplan, *The Age of the Universe: A Torah True Perspective* (Rueven Meir Caplan, 2008).

[16]   Alexander Poltorak, "On the Age of the Universe," BOr HaTorah Vol. 13, ed. Prof. Herman Branover (Israel: SHAMIR, 1999). Dr. Poltorak performs the calculation assuming the same two periods of time. His first period is a protophysical period, and the second, once man becomes the conscious observer and collapses the wave function, is a physical period. Although it does not affect the calculations, this author considers the first period to be physical (e.g., the sun is a physical object on Day 4) because God is the conscious observer during this period. When man arrives, he takes over the conscious observer role and determines

what happens on earth from then on (according to his "clock"). God hides and allows man to exercise his free will.

[17]   Alexander Poltorak, "The Age of the Universe Using the Many-Worlds Interpretation," BOr HaTorah Vol. 18, ed. Prof. Herman Branover (Israel: SHAMIR, 2008).

[18]   Gerald L. Schroeder, *The Science of God: The Convergence of Scientific and Biblical Wisdom* (New York: Broadway Books, 1997), Chapter 3. This work looks in science for the conversion factor based on the scientific measurement of the rate of expansion of the universe, which has the effect of stretching the six days of creation.

Chapter 2

Divergent Points of View: The Origins Debate

The creation-evolution controversy[1] (or the origins debate) is a recurring cultural, political, and theological dispute about the origins of the earth, life, humanity, and the universe. The dispute continues between those who espouse religious belief and thus support a creationist view, versus those who accept evolution as supported by scientific consensus. The dispute particularly involves the field of evolutionary biology, in addition to fields such as geology, paleontology, and cosmology. As will be seen in this chapter, the dispute has had serious negative consequences on society.

A divisive element in the dispute relates to the timeline matter: 6,000 years versus 13.7 billion years. Solving the timeline discrepancy will, it is hoped, foster a renewed dialogue between science and religion and thereby avoid a repetition of some unfortunate history described herein. To this end, important questions will be raised. What if the scriptures themselves argued for an epoch interpretation? What if they provided an exact timeline? And what if this timeline matched the scientific timeline surprisingly well?

Many people think deeply about the universal questions of origins, and particularly how these questions affect their own lives. Genesis remains of special importance to Christians and Jews because they accept that account as the revealed Word of God.

Scientific Inquiry

Beginnings

Scientific inquiry began with the ancient Greeks. Although many Greeks retained religious beliefs about nature, some Greek philosophers proposed theories about the physical world based on reason. For example, Thales (circa 585 B.C.) decided that the natural world was founded on a series of interconnecting physical laws, rather than random chance or divine providence. Empedocles (circa 450 B.C.) identified the four basic natural elements of fire, water, air, and earth and declared them to be eternal in nature. Plato expanded on the claims of Empedocles by indicating the four elements can be combined in a nearly infinite number of ways to create various substances. Plato also believed the planets must move in some kind of circuitous order, setting the stage for later scientific study of planetary motion. However, Plato felt that God had indeed created the universe. Eratosthenes (276 B.C.–194 B.C.) coined the term "geography" and made the first accurate measurement of the earth's circumference. He also is credited with calculating a roughly accurate distance between the earth and sun; he likewise invented the leap day, now common to our calendars. Since the classical Greco-Roman era, humankind has continued to ponder the origins of the universe and the very beginning of life itself.

Questions revolving around the role of science in our origins reached a new zenith during the Renaissance, when science assumed a dominant role in cultural and educational forums. Nicholas Copernicus (1473–1543) observed that the earth moves around the sun, using a formula to estimate the positions of other planets. Tycho Brahe (1546–1601) was a Danish astronomer who catalogued more than 1,000 stars. Johan Kepler (1571–1630) expanded on Brahe's views and observed that heavenly bodies follow well-defined orbits that obey simple mathematical rules.

As science advanced, religious authority, particularly that of the Catholic Church, began to wane. Great thinkers and religious minds enlarged their vision of the universe to encompass a longer time span from the beginning of matter to the current era. As religious authority broke down during the 1700s, natural philosophers struggled even more insistently to devise purely materialistic explanations for life.

An Old Earth

Around 1800, British civil engineer William Smith began documenting, for the first time, dramatic differences in the fossils found within specific layers of rock strata. Each era of rock formation appeared to have its own unique population of creatures. These discoveries in geology led to various theories of an ancient earth, and fossils revealing past extinctions prompted realization of evolutionary possibilities. Those who believed in the Genesis creation account responded to the old earth evidence by interpreting the six days of creation as six epochs. This adaptation of the timelines allowed the dialogue between science and religion to continue.

Evolution

The widespread acceptance of Pierre Simon Laplace's nebular hypothesis (a model explaining the formation and evolution of the solar system) established an evolutionary view of cosmic origins as early as the late 1700s. The idea of organic evolution was widely disseminated by the early 1800s.

In 1858, after learning that naturalist Alfred Wallace had independently hit on the same idea, Charles Darwin, who had been working on his theory of natural selection for many years, finally announced his theory and published *On the Origin of Species* a year later. This book revolutionized biological thought.

On the Origin of Species started an ongoing revolution in human thought. In the work Darwin does not prove his theory of evolution by natural selection. Rather, he argues that it is a better explanation for the origin of organic species[2] than creationism. The implications of Darwin's theory provoked immediate controversy. Although accepting his theory did not preclude belief in God, it did allow proponents to dispense with the need to believe in a supernatural creator of species or a literal interpretation of the Genesis creation account. Further, it undermined natural theology (man as a special creation) by suggesting that species evolve through random chance and a struggle for survival. Crucially, the theory required billions of years to work (i.e., for species to evolve), not just six days.

From that point, the idea of evolution gained ascendancy in Western biology. It offered a plausible explanation for the origin of all species and raised a host of new issues for scientific study. By 1875, virtually all biologists in Europe and America had adopted an evolutionary view of origins.

Even as biologists accepted the basic theory of evolution, they came to doubt the sufficiency of Darwin's idea that the evolutionary process proceeded through random inborn variations selected by a competitive struggle for survival. Alternative mechanisms for evolution were considered, although an enhanced version of Darwin's theory proved ultimately right in the end.

Although by 1900 most Western biologists and intellectuals accepted some theory of evolution, popular and religious opposition lingered. Technical arguments that appealed to scientists failed to persuade the public, particularly when it came to the notion that humans had evolved from apes. The fossil record became a barrier to widespread acceptance of scientific ideas. Opponents decried the lack of fossils linking either major biological types (such as reptiles and mammals) or humans to their alleged simian ancestors. Deeply religious folk rejected all challenges to the literal biblical account of a six-day creation.

Genetics

Even evolutionists were mired in doubts and disagreement at the dawn of the twentieth century. Biologists still believed that evolution had occurred, but there was no consensus among them on how it operated. All options seemed inadequate, especially classical Darwinism. Then, as often happens in science, answers came from an unexpected source—genetics.

By the 1940s, consensus emerged among biologists on how the evolutionary process worked. Evolution was a purely materialistic process driven by the natural selection of random variation at the genetic level. This so-called neo-Darwinian synthesis was more fully Darwinian than Darwin's own conclusions. The breakthrough was largely conceptual; evolution, or at least the mechanism by which it operates, was and remains an unproven theory at the macroscopic level (i.e., species changing into other, very different species).

Abuses of Eugenics

During the period from the late 1800s until 1940, while scientists struggled with an evolutionary method, evolutionary thinking in biology spilled over into social thought.

Coupled with a rudimentary appreciation of genetics, proponents of social Darwinism fostered the eugenics movement, a crusade advocating the procreation of more children from genetically fit parents and fewer children from genetically unfit ones. Proponents typically equated fitness with intelligence, but they often favored physical strength, health, and beauty as well. Some of their methods called for voluntary participation, but many nations and most American states enacted at least some compulsory eugenic laws before the movement was discredited by Nazi practices during World War II.

The positive eugenics movement encouraged the fittest parents to reproduce in order to give birth to the strongest, healthiest offspring. Respected leaders like Winston Churchill and Theodore Roosevelt, among other prominent politicians, expressed concern that professional social classes were not reproducing in sufficient numbers. Progressive sociologist Edward A. Ross referred to this vein of thought as "race suicide." Educational programs were developed to teach students the importance of eugenic mate selection as well as the civic duty of bearing children. Earlier anti-miscegenation laws were revived. Societies that adopted eugenic values sponsored "fitter family" and "eugenic baby" contests. It was even proposed that eugenic fitness be established as a marriage prerequisite, and the value was in fact adopted as a policy by certain liberal Protestant churches. Some countries adopted tax and unemployment policies to encourage able citizens to have children. Alternatively, the aim of negative eugenics was fewer children from those considered to be unfit.

The movement grew to such proportions that American states and most Western nations adopted policies of sexually segregating specific dysgenic classes, especially the mentally retarded. Thirty-five American states and several European countries enacted policies to sexually sterilize the mentally ill and retarded, along with habitual criminals and epileptics. Germany's program was later expanded to include Jews.

Approximately 60,000 Americans were sterilized under compulsory state programs. These programs were upheld as constitutional by the U.S. Supreme Court in 1927. Partly on eugenic grounds, Congress limited immigration of non-Nordic races. Nazi Germany progressed from eugenic sterilization to euthanasia. German geneticists aggressively supported racial purity programs. More biologists than any other professional group joined the Nazi Party.

Except for the Catholic Church, opposition to eugenics was disorganized and ineffective until the late 1930s, when Nazi practices grew to alarming proportions and discredited all such efforts. At about the same time, social scientists increasingly began to examine environmental causes of human behavior. Nurture replaced nature in social scientific thought. Gradually, geneticists recognized the complexity of human heredity. Simple eugenic remedies were abandoned as ways to deal with multi-factorial traits. By the end of World War II, social Darwinism was morally bankrupt.

Creationism

Decades of popular concern over the theory of evolution erupted during the 1920s into a movement by conservative American Protestants against teaching evolution in public schools. The movement was part of their larger effort to defend traditional beliefs and values against liberalism in the church and secularism in society. The movement met immediate opposition from religious liberals and a broad array of secularists. The battle was joined over the theory of evolution because both sides viewed it as central to religious liberalism and scientific secularism. The battle reached its public climax in 1925, when Tennessee's new law against teaching evolution was challenged by a schoolteacher named John Scopes. The ensuing court case helped turn the issue into a flashpoint for public controversy. The anti-evolution statute was upheld as constitutional. Other American states and school districts imposed similar measures.

Scientific Creationism

After the commemoration of the centennial of Darwin's *On the Origin of Species* in 1959, scientists hailed the triumph of a consensus theory of evolution. Scientists largely ignored the persistent anti-evolutionism that marked conservative Christianity in America, and assumed that it would die. However, the Judeo-Christian religious sectors had drifted toward a more literal interpretation of the Bible as the Word of God, and the six days of creation as literal 24-hour days. Coupled with the rise of Neo-Darwinism, this movement heightened tensions between traditional religious beliefs and modern scientific thought. Those tensions underlay the phenomenal impact of *The Genesis Flood*[3], a 1961 book that argues scientific evidence supports the biblical account of creation. Unaccepted and not supported by the scientific community, it nonetheless became known as scientific creationism.

Scientific creationism swept through America's conservative Protestant churches during the 1960s and 1970s, reviving belief that God had created the universe and all species in the past 10,000 years. Rather than simply opposing evolution theory, believers now offered an alternative view for inclusion in public education. With the rise of the Christian Right in American politics, creationists imposed this theory in many areas until 1987, when the U.S. Supreme Court overturned creationist instruction as violating the Constitutional separation of church and state. One by one, each curriculum teaching scientific creationism was struck down as unconstitutional, culminating in a 1987 U.S. Supreme Court ruling against Louisiana's Balanced Treatment Act. The Court ruled that no law was needed to teach scientific evidence for or against evolution; therefore, this law must have been passed to promote religion. These rulings ended the teaching of scientific creationism in public schools.

Among the ten percent of Americans who rejects divine intervention as having a part in our origins, a purely neo-Darwinian struggle for survival among randomly mutating genes replaces purposeful design as the source of life's diversity. Others in this camp, such as paleontologist Stephen Jay Gould (who died in 2002 but whose influence remains strong), believe the neo-Darwinian synthesis needs refinement to account for evolution yet remain confident that wholly materialistic mechanisms, still to be discovered, can do so.

Creationists counter that evolution remains unproven. They maintain that alternative ideas (or at least scientific objections to materialism) belong in the classroom. Even many Americans who reject scientific creationism agree that an intelligent designer should not automatically be ruled out as the source of life and individual species. In America, the debate over origins remains as intense as ever, as does the controversy over the timelines.

Theistic Evolution

Lost in the polarized conflict between materialistic evolution and special creation are those who accept that earthly species evolve and see a role for God in that process. Broadly speaking, this is theistic evolution.

Some Darwinists also believe that certain human traits, such as love and consciousness, were specially created in evolved hominids to form humans. The Catholic Church accepts this position.

Between theistic evolutionists and special creationists are self-identified progressive creationists. They believe that God intervened at various points in the geologic past to create the basic life forms that then evolved into the various species we know today.

Half of all Americans do not accept any significant role for evolution in the generation of different kinds of plants and animals. At most, they accept the so-called micro-evolution of nearly similar species, such as Darwin's finches on the Galapagos Islands.

Intelligent Design

During the 1990s, a loosely organized group of Christian scholars advanced the idea that species are simply too complex to evolve. While eschewing biblical arguments and chronologies, they saw species as the product of intelligent design. Some in this group stress that science should not *a priori* exclude supernatural causes for natural phenomena; gaps and abrupt appearances in the fossil record are best explained by special creation.

Current Situation

Nearly 150 years after the publication of Darwin's theory of evolution by natural selection, it remains central to the scientific and popular debate over organic origins. Scientists generally accept and push its applications. Many others see it as flawed. The abrupt nature of the fossil record, in particular the Cambrian explosion which shows a sudden beginning to complex life in a very short period, and the existence of traits such as love and consciousness, remain to some explainable only by creationism.

The division is partly underlined by an inability to reconcile the stories (i.e., the scientific account via the Big Bang and the fossil record as opposed to the Genesis account) on a common timeline. Many have by now abandoned the early six-epoch view of Genesis (now known as old earth creationism[4]) and moved toward an interpretation of a literal six days (now known as young earth creationism[5]), with most scientists maintaining a strict view of evolution, over billions of years, with no room for God.

Today, the origins debate, which has historically been prominent in the United States, is spilling into other countries. In Europe the Committee on Culture, Science and Education of the Parliamentary Assembly of the Council of Europe recently issued a report on the attempt by American-inspired creationists to promote creationism in European schools. The report states:

> If we are not careful, creationism could become a threat to human rights which are a key concern of the Council of Europe.... The war on the theory of evolution and on its proponents most often originates in forms of religious extremism which are closely allied to extreme right-wing political movements... some advocates of creationism are out to replace democracy by theocracy.[6]

In the Islamic world the situation is mixed.[7] In Egypt, evolution is currently taught in schools. But Saudi Arabia and Sudan have both banned the teaching of evolution. Scientific creationism has also been heavily promoted in Turkey and in immigrant Muslim communities in Western Europe. In Israel the debate also continues, as illustrated below in a 2010 newspaper report:

The Education Ministry's chief scientist sparked a furor Saturday with remarks questioning the reliability of evolution: "If textbooks state explicitly that human beings' origins are to be found with monkeys, I would want students to pursue and grapple with other opinions. There are many people who don't believe the evolutionary account is correct," he said.[8]

In America the general public remains divided by the origins debate. Surveys (see Table 2.1[9]) indicate that about half the population believes that God specially created the first humans. Most of the rest affirm that God guided evolution. About 15% accept the God-less theory of origins that dominates science.

The timeline issue remains a component of the origins debate worldwide.

Table 2.1 Creation vs. Evolution—Beliefs in America

Belief system	Creationist view	Theistic evolution	Evolution
Beliefs	God created man pretty much in his present form at one time within the last 10,000 years.	Man has developed over millions of years from less advanced forms of life, but God guided this process, including man's creation.	Man has developed over millions of years from less advanced forms of life. God had no part in this process.
Year			
1982-JUL	44%	38%	9%
1993-JUN	47%	35%	11%
1997-NOV	44%	39%	10%
1999-AUG	47%	40%	9%
2001-FEB	45%	37%	12%
2004-NOV	45%	38%	13%
2007-MAY	43%	38%	14%
2012-MAY	46%	32%	15%

[1]   Edward J. Larson, *The Theory of Evolution: A History of Controversy* (U.S.A.: The Teaching Company, 2002).

[2]   Charles Darwin, *On the Origin of Species* (Cambridge: Harvard University Press, 1964).

[3]   John C. Whitcomb and Henry M. Morris, *The Genesis Flood* (NJ: Presbyterian and Reformed Publishing Co., 1961).

[4]   Old earth creationism (OEC) is an umbrella term for a number of creationism proponents. Their worldview is typically more compatible with mainstream scientific thought on the issues

of geology, cosmology, and the age of the earth, particularly in comparison to young earth creationism; nevertheless, OEC adherents still generally take the accounts of creation in Genesis more literally (albeit accepting the six-epoch view) than those who abide by theistic evolution (also known as evolutionary creationism) in that OEC rejects the scientific consensus accepting evolution.

[5] Young earth creationism (YEC) is a form of creationism that asserts the heavens, earth, and all life were created by direct acts of God during a relatively short period, sometime between 5,700 and 10,000 years ago. Its adherents believe that God created the earth in six 24-hour days, taking a literal interpretation of the Genesis creation narrative as a basis for their beliefs.

[6] Council of Europe, Parliamentary Assembly, Resolution 1580 (2007), *The Dangers of Creationism in Education*, Text adopted by the Assembly on 4 October 2007 (35th Sitting) (see Doc. 11375, report of the Committee on Culture, Science and Education, rapporteur: Mrs. Brasseur).

[7] Stephen Jones, "In the Beginning: The Debate over Creation and Evolution, Once Most Conspicuous in America, is Fast Going Global," *The Economist*, 19 April 2007.

[8] Or Kashti, Zafrir Rinat, "Scientists Irate after Top Education Official Questions Evolution," Haaretz.com, 29 December 2010.

[9] (i) "Reading the Polls on Evolution and Creationism," Pew Research Center Pollwatch, 28 September 2005.

(ii) "Evolution, Creationism, Intelligent Design," Gallup Inc., 14 July 2012, www.gallup.com/poll/21814/evolution-creationism-intelligent-design.aspx. The small difference between the total and 100% owes to "don't know" response.

Chapter 3

The Science Answer

Has the scientific method produced a timeline for the development of the universe and the appearance of life on earth?

If so, how complete is this information?

The Big Bang theory is the scientific answer that explains and provides a timeline for the development of our universe. This well-tested theory is one of the most remarkable successes of modern science.

Evolution is the scientific theory to explain the appearance of life on earth. The fossil record documents the history of the appearance of life on earth. Fossils paint a clear picture of the timeline for the appearance of life over the past 3.5 billion years. This account is a record that is independent of any theory, such as evolution, because it simply documents the timing of fossils as they are discovered, categorized, and dated.

The purpose of this chapter is to examine what both the Big Bang theory and the fossil record findings tell us about the timeline for the development of the universe and the appearance of life on earth. The information in this chapter summarizes the current state (as at 2011) of scientific knowledge, relying upon peer reviewed articles and books written by well-known scientists.

As discussed in Chapter 1, the scientific method provides a robust way to measure things (such as the age of bones) and to develop explanations and theories of our universe and the world. Over time, the scientific method has been proved to arrive at correct results, as long as these results can be tested. The scientific method has consistently yielded outstandingly accurate and useful results on which we rely, and in fact trust, in our lives every day. There is no reason to doubt the fundamental accuracy of the body of knowledge comprising the Big Bang theory and the age and nature of the fossil record, although refinements continue to emerge on a routine basis.

A comparison of the Genesis creation narrative to scientific findings cannot be made without first understanding that tested theories and measurements produced by the scientific method are by and large accurate.

The Big Bang Theory

Overview

What is known as the Big Bang is the prevailing cosmological theory of the universe's origins and development. According to the Big Bang model, the universe, originally in an extremely hot and dense state, expanded rapidly. It has since cooled by continuing to expand to its present diluted state. Based on the best available measurements, scientists have determined the original state of the universe existed about 13.7 billion years ago.[1] The theory offers the most accurate, logical explanation supported by current scientific evidence and observations.

This model of cosmology rests on two key ideas that date back to the early 20th century: general relativity and the cosmological principle. General relativity—or the general theory of relativity —is the theory of gravitation published by Albert Einstein in 1915. It remains the consensus in modern physics, providing a unified description of gravity as a geometric property of space and time.

The cosmological principle is the working assumption that observers on earth do not occupy a restrictive, unusual or privileged location within the universe and thus, there are no preferred directions or places in the universe. This means that all the matter in the universe is on average distributed uniformly.

Taking under consideration the law of gravity and formulating an assumption about how matter is distributed, the next step is to assess the dynamics of the universe—how space and the matter within it evolves over time. The details depend on further information about matter in the universe, namely its density (mass per unit volume) and its pressure (force it exerts per unit area). But the generic picture that emerges is that the universe started from a very small volume with an initial expansion rate. For the most part, this rate of expansion has been slowing (decelerating) due to the gravitational pull of the matter on itself. However, recently this expansion has begun to accelerate owing to the effect of hypothesized dark energy, which has the opposite effect of gravity (i.e., it causes matter to separate).

Tuning the Theory to Match Observations[2]

Today, we can accurately measure large properties of the universe with space-based and land-based instruments. Using these measurements, we can determine a dozen or so cosmological parameters that define the properties of the universe. When these parameters are used in the Big Bang theory, the theory predicts results that match current observations.

Five key sets of observations comprise the measurements that are used to determine the cosmological parameters:

(1) distance measurements to nearby stars

(2) distance measurements to remote astronomical objects

(3) microwave background (i.e., radiation left over from an early stage in the development of the universe) and its sound spectrum

(4) maps of how fast the galaxies are moving

(5) light element abundances (i.e., ratio in which the lightest elements are present in the universe).

Although each of the above measures only one or two parameters, when combined they form an amazingly powerful tool for measuring all cosmological parameters to a high level of precision. The best-fitting parameter set is called the concordance model. It is the remarkable ability of completely different observational sets to zero in on the same parameter values that has led to an endorsement of the Big Bang theory by the scientific community.

After the parameters are determined, the Big Bang model is calculated by computer to predict and date events from the beginning of time until now.

The Timeline Predicted by the Big Bang Theory

The theory develops a very detailed technical timeline for the first several seconds of the universe's existence, which however will not be reproduced here as this involves a level of detail that is not obtained from the biblical Genesis account.

The following text (Table 3.1) describes the development of the universe as predicted by the theory, indicating the time frame as a sequence from the beginning (at time zero) until now, and describing the main observable events at each time period.

Table 3.1 Timeline for the Development of the Universe

Time	Description
The first three minutes Early phase of the Big Bang[3]	From an initial condensed energy mass, space and time, forces of physics, and the elementary particles are formed, including dark matter and normal matter building blocks. As will be seen later, all parameters of the universe are some-how tuned miraculously to create an inhabitable universe.
Three minutes Hydrogen appears	As the universe expands, the temperature falls to the point where atomic nuclei can begin to form. Protons (hydrogen ions) and neutrons begin to combine into atomic nuclei in the process of nuclear fusion. However, this only lasts about seventeen minutes, after which time the temperature and density of the universe have fallen to the point where nuclear fusion cannot continue. At this time, there is about three times more hydrogen than helium-4 (by mass) and only trace quantities of other nuclei. All other elements in the universe are formed much later due to nuclear reactions in stars—a process known as nucleosynthesis.
5–200 MY (million years) The Dark Age	By 5 MY, most photons (light) are in the infra-red spectrum and the universe appears dark. Atomic gas continues to fall toward the dark matter clumps, which grow more pronounced. Near 100 MY, the densest clumps halt their expansion and begin collapsing (due to their own weight). By 200 MY the first mini-halos of dark matter form, and within these the atomic gas cools and collapses to make the first stars, whose light brings the Dark Age to a close.

Time	Description
200–800 MY First stars and the epoch of re-ionization	Because the first stars contain pristine gas, they are massive, luminous, hot, and short-lived (about 1 MY in lifetime) compared to today's stars (our sun is expected to last 10 BY). They are quite strongly grouped because they form where peaks in density line up for all scales. They die in supernova explosions, releasing heavy elements (establishing the rest of the periodic table via the process of nucleosynthesis) that pollute the surrounding gas. The strong radiation from the first stars, and possibly the first quasars, ionize much of the remaining neutral hydrogen and helium in the universe. This makes the whole universe appear to be a giant neon sign. Light is everywhere (i.e., no dark patches in the sky).
1–2 BY Infant galaxies	Star groups merge to form infant galaxies. This time is characterized by frequent galaxy collisions, high star birth rates, and high supernova rates. Heavy elements production changes the pattern of star formation, reducing their mass, making them less luminous and longer lived, more like today's stars. The universe is no longer completely lit up; it now comprises bright star-filled areas as well as dark areas.

Time	Description
2–3 BY Star birth and quasar peak	The star birth rate reaches its maximum, as does the formation and feeding of super-massive black holes, and much of the visible universe is made. After this point in time there is still star birth and death, but the rate of star formation decreases rapidly with time and eventually reaches today's very low level of star birth rate.
5–8 BY Galaxy formation continues	The first rich galaxy clusters form by 5 BY. The formation of the Milky Way's disk,[4] from which the solar system is made, occurs at about 5.5 BY. The first modern spiral galaxies have formed by 8 BY.
9 BY Formation of the solar system	The solar system[5] (i.e., sun and planets) forms.
13.7 BY Today	The theory predicts that 13.7 BY is the time elapsed since the beginning until now, i.e., the age of the universe.

The Fine Tuning Problem

Although the theory does a good job of matching observations and provides a detailed description of events, many of which can be verified, it struggles with a problem. If we vary almost any of the particular properties of the universe, or the laws of physics and their parameters, by a very modest amount, the universe cannot exist. This is the fine tuning problem.[6] Why do the universe's parameters exist in a narrow life-giving range? There is no generally accepted scientific answer.

How would the universe differ if the parameters were different? To find out, imagine what happens when we change, one by one, the starting parameters. Here are some examples:

1. An atom is composed of a nucleus surrounded by electrons. The nucleus is made up of protons and neutrons. Protons are just 0.2% lighter than neutrons. If we reverse this, atoms collapse because electrons combine with protons to make neutrons, and the universe contains just chunks of neutron matter—no life. If neutrons were 10% heavier than protons, they would decay into protons, causing nuclei to disintegrate. With no nuclei, there is no chemistry. And no life.

2. What about the initial distribution of matter in the universe? Matter is quite uniform; nonetheless, it has a small structure, or roughness (think of it as ripples), from which galaxies eventually emerge. If you were to enlarge the roughness by ten times, huge black holes would form, but no galaxies. If you were to shrink the roughness by ten times (i.e., make it very smooth), galaxies might never form, and planets never emerge.

3. What if we were to change space and/or time dimensions (an *a priori* initial condition)? Simulations find either chaotic and unstable behavior or extremely simple behavior, with no richness. Only one time and three space dimensions provide stable behavior rich in possibilities.

4. What if we vary the strength of the strong force that binds nuclei together? Turn it up, and all hydrogen combines in the minute-old universe, so there's no hydrogen for stars to burn, and none to make water. Turn it down, and deuterium (an isotope of hydrogen) is unstable. Without deuterium, heavier elements cannot form, and we have no planets or people.

In summary, once the starting parameters are established, the Big Bang theory produces an accurate and detailed timeline of the development of the universe that matches scientific observations.

The Fossil Record

What Is the Fossil Record?

Fossils (from Latin *fossus*, literally "having been dug up") are the preserved remains or traces of animals, plants, and other organisms from the remote past. The accumulation of fossils, both discovered and undiscovered, and their placement in fossil-containing rock formations and sedimentary layers (strata) is known as the fossil record. The study of fossils across geological time, how they were formed, and the evolutionary relationships between them are key functions of paleontology.

The fossil record depicts life's history as it unfolded over the span of 3.5 billion years.

Evidence of Life Preserved in the Fossil Record

Fossils can be microscopic, such as single bacterial cells only one micrometer in diameter, or gigantic, such as dinosaurs and trees many meters long and weighing many tons. A fossil normally contains only a portion of the deceased organism, usually the portion that was partially mineralized during life, such as the bones and teeth of vertebrates, or the protective external skeletons of invertebrates. Fossils may also consist of marks left behind by the organism while it was alive, such as a footprint or feces. These are called trace fossils.

Dating the Fossil Record

Since the early twentieth century, absolute dating methods, such as radiometric dating (including potassium/argon, argon/argon, uranium series, and, for very recent fossils, carbon14 dating), have been used to verify the relative ages of fossils and to provide absolute ages for many fossils. Radiometric dating has shown that the earliest known fossils are more than 3.4 billion years old. Various dating methods continue in use today. Despite some variance in these dating methods, they offer evidence for a very old earth, a planet of approximately 4.6 billion years.

Radioactive dating compares the amount of a naturally occurring radioactive isotope and its decay products, using known decay rates. All ordinary matter combines chemical elements, each with its own atomic number, indicating the number of protons in the atomic nucleus. Additionally, elements may exist in different isotopes, with each differing in the number of neutrons in the nucleus. A particular isotope of an element is called a nuclide. Some nuclides are inherently unstable. Eventually, an atom of such a nuclide will spontaneously decay (i.e., radioactively decay) into a different nuclide.

While the exact time at which a particular nucleus decays is unpredictable, a collection of radioactive nuclide atoms decays at a rate described by a parameter known as the half-life, usually given in units of years. After one half-life has elapsed, half of the nuclide's atoms will have decayed into a daughter nuclide or decay product. Often, the daughter nuclide is radioactive, leading to the formation of another daughter nuclide, and eventually to a stable (non-radioactive) daughter nuclide; each step in this chain-like process is characterized by a distinct half-life. Usually the half-life of interest in radiometric dating is the longest in the chain, which is the rate-limiting factor in the ultimate transformation of the radioactive nuclide into its stable daughter. Isotopic systems that have been used for radiometric dating have half-lives ranging from only about ten years (e.g., tritium) to many thousands of years (e.g., carbon 14), to a billion years (e.g., potassium-argon), and to even longer periods of time.

Can We Trust the Results of Radiometric Dating?

A nuclide's half-life depends on its nuclear properties; it is not affected by external factors such as temperature, pressure, chemical environment, or presence of a magnetic or electric field. Nuclear properties and, therefore, the half-life of nuclides have re-mained stable as the earth has evolved and undergone volcanism and weathering (even the flood described in Genesis). Given this stability in materials containing a radioactive nuclide, the propor-tion of original nuclide to its decay product(s) has changed in a predictable way due to the effects of decay over time. In this way the abundance of related nuclides can be used as a clock to meas-ure time between the incorporation of the original nuclide(s) into a material to the present.

Thus, fossils containing or surrounded by radioactive material include their own nuclear clock. When we uncover the fossil today, we can read its age. Similar methods help us keep time (for exam-ple, nuclear clocks) for our most advanced systems nowadays — from GPS satellite positioning to weapons.

The Sequence of Life Revealed in the Fossil Record

By synthesizing the fossil record, classifying fossils, determin-ing their age, and placing them in the context of the geologic scale, scientists have revealed the sequence of life on earth:

1. The fossil record begins with 3.5 to 3.0 billion-year-old rocks from Australia and South Africa, in which are preserved the remains of blue-green algae. In rocks more than a billion years old, only fossils of single-celled organisms are found. In rocks that are about 550 million years old, fossils of simple, multi-cellular animals can be found. At 530 million years ago (Ma) there is an explosion of life, followed by the gradual appearance of new animals—yet each within relatively short and even abrupt time frames: fish with jaws 400 million years ago, amphibians 350 million years ago, rep-tiles 300 million years ago, mammals 230 million years ago, and birds 150 million years ago.[7] The detailed timeline revealed by the fossil record is shown in Table 3.2.

2. Fossilization is rare. Scientists have unearthed only 250,000 fossil species. Given the vast number of species throughout history, this is a remarkably small fraction. Indeed, the millions of species alive today constitute but approximately one percent of all species that have existed.

3. In some cases, the record can be interpreted to show that certain organisms progressed systematically over time, each version displaying what appears to be a modification over the earlier. In other cases, there are large gaps in the fossil record, and the developmental process for some organisms is not as clear. Often, organisms lead to a dead end. Some scientists believe they have found some transitional forms.[8] Others have seen a much more punctuated evolutionary process in the record, as did the American paleontologist and evolutionary biologist Stephen Jay Gould. "Every once in a while, a more complex creature appears. But the additions are rare and episodic. They do not even constitute an evolutionary series but form a motley sequence of distantly related taxa, usually depicted as eukaryotic cell, jellyfish, trilobite, nautiloid, eurypterid (a large relative of horseshoe crabs), fish, an amphibian such as Eryops, a dinosaur, a mammal and a human being."[9]

4. Throughout geologic time, life was punctuated by distinct events. Large numbers of organisms appeared in a short time span, and periodically mass extinctions occurred, such as at the end of the Cretaceous Period, when a majority of species came to an end over a relatively short time period.

5. Life remained mostly unicellular for the first five-sixths of its history—from the first recorded fossils at 3.5 billion years to the first well-documented multi-cellular animals less than 600 million years ago. Then the record shows the remarkable Cambrian explosion during which all but one modern phylum of animal life made a first appearance in the fossil record. The phylum level of biological classification corresponds to a group of organisms with a cer-

tain degree of morphological or developmental similarity. Morphology includes aspects of the outward appearance (shape, structure, color, and pattern) as well as the form and structure of internal parts, like bones and organs. Since the Cambrian explosion, "although interesting and portentous events have occurred since, from the flowering of dinosaurs to the origin of human consciousness, we do not exaggerate greatly in stating that the subsequent history of animal life amounts to little more than variations on anatomical themes established during the Cambrian explosion within five million years."[10] Others have argued that the Cambrian explosion might have lasted as long as 50 million years and that some significant phyla may have appeared later in time.[11]

In conclusion, the fossil record depicts the history of life on earth. The picture reveals the appearance of very simple life forms one billion years (BY) after the earth formed, followed by little activity for billions of years, with complex life appearing in a remarkably short time—about 500 million years ago, followed by further appearance of many life forms and several mass extinctions as well.

Table 3.2 Timeline for Appearance of Life on Earth[12]

Time	Fossil record activity
3.5 BY ago	The oldest fossils of single-celled organisms date from this time.
2.4 BY ago	The great oxidation event, when oxygen begins to build in the atmosphere.
2.2 BY ago	Fossil evidence emerges of blue-green algae and of photosynthesis: the ability to take in sunlight and carbon dioxide and obtain energy, releasing oxygen as a by-product.
900 Ma?	The first multi-cellular life develops around this time.
630 Ma	Some animals show bilateral symmetry for the first time: that is, they now have a defined top and bottom, as well as a front and back.

Time	Fossil record activity
565 Ma	Fossilized animal trails suggest that some creatures are moving on their own.
535 Ma	The Cambrian explosion begins, with many new body forms appearing.
530 Ma	The first true vertebrate appears—an animal with a backbone. Around the same time, the first clear trilobite fossils appear. These invertebrates look like oversized woodlice and grow to 70 centimeters in length.
500 Ma	Fossil evidence shows that animals were exploring land at this time.
489 Ma	The Great Ordovician Biodiversification Event begins, leading to an increase in diversity. Within each major group of animals and plants, many new varieties appear.
460 Ma	Fish split into two major groups: bony fish and cartilaginous fish. The cartilaginous fish, as the name implies, have skeletons made of cartilage rather than harder bone. They eventually include all sharks, skates, and rays.
450 Ma	Two extinction events occur. Together they are ranked by many scientists as the second largest of five major extinctions in earth's history.
425 Ma	First primitive macroscopic plants appear on land.
400 Ma	The oldest known insect lives around this time.
397 Ma	The first four-limbed animals, or tetrapods, emerge in the fossil record. The tetrapods give rise to all amphibians, reptiles, birds, and mammals.
385 Ma	The oldest fossilized tree dates from this period.
375 Ma	Late Devonian extinction—a prolonged series of extinctions—eliminates a vast number of species.

Time	Fossil record activity
340 Ma	The first major split occurs in the tetrapods, with the amphibians branching off.
310 Ma	Within the remaining tetrapods, the sauropsids and synapsids split from each other. The sauropsids include all modern reptiles, plus dinosaurs and birds. The first synapsids are also reptiles, but with distinctive jaws. Mammals are believed to be their descendants.
250 Ma	The Permian period ends with the greatest mass extinction in earth's history, wiping out great swathes of species, including the last of the trilobites. The ecosystem recovers and undergoes a fundamental shift. Whereas before the synapsids dominated, the sauropsids now take over—most famously in the form of dinosaurs. Ancestors of mammals survive as small, nocturnal creatures. In the oceans, the ammonites, cousins of the modern nautilus and octopus, appear. Several groups of reptiles occupy the seas, developing into the great marine reptiles of the dinosaur era.
215 Ma	First mammals appear.
210 Ma	Bird-like footprints are found in this era.
205 Ma	As the Triassic period ends, another mass extinction strikes, allowing dinosaurs to take over from their sauropsid cousins. Proto-mammals with warm-bloodedness—the ability to maintain their internal temperature, regardless of external conditions—appear.

Time	Fossil record activity
180 Ma	The first split occurs in the early mammal population. A group of mammals that lay eggs rather than giving birth to live young breaks apart from the others. Few survive today; they include the duck-billed platypus and the echidnas.
150 Ma	Archaeopteryx, the famous first bird, lives in Europe.
140 Ma	Around this time, placental mammals split from their cousins the marsupials. Marsupials, like the modern kangaroo, give birth when the babies are very small, but nourish them in a pouch for the first few weeks or months of life. The majority of modern marsupials live in Australia, which they reach by a roundabout route. Originating in southeast Asia, they spread into North America (which was attached to Asia at the time), then to South America and Antarctica before making the final journey to Australia about 50 million years ago.
130 Ma	The first flowering plants emerge, following a period of rapid evolution.
105 to 85 Ma	The placental mammals split into four major groups: the laurasiatheres (a hugely diverse group including all hoofed mammals, whales, bats, and dogs); the euarchontoglires (primates, rodents, and others); Xenarthra (including anteaters and armadillos); and afrotheres (elephants, aardvarks, and others).
100 Ma	The Cretaceous dinosaurs peak in size.
65 Ma	The Cretaceous-Tertiary (K/T) extinction wipes out several species, including all giant reptiles: the dinosaurs, pterosaurs, ichthyosaurs, and plesiosaurs. The ammonites are also wiped out. The extinction clears the way for mammals, which go on to dominate the planet.

Time	Fossil record activity
63 Ma	The primates split into two groups: dry-nosed primates and wet-nosed primates.
55 Ma	The Paleocene/Eocene extinction results from a sudden rise in greenhouse gases that sends temperatures soaring and transforms the planet, wiping out many species in the depths of the sea—though sparing species in shallow seas and on land.

---

[1]   (i) Results from NASA's Wilkinson Microwave Anisotropy Probe (WMAP) satellite, launched in 2001, set the age of the universe at 13.7 billion years plus or minus 130 million years. Cosmological models based on the Hubble constant (such as ΛCDM) result in a 13.73 billion year-old universe.
Refer to http://map.gsfc.nasa.gov/universe/uni_age.html.

(ii) Gary F. Hinshaw, et al, "Five-Year Wilkinson Microwave Anisotropy Probe Observations: Data Processing, Sky Maps, and Basic Results," *The Astrophysical Journal Supplement* 180/2 (2009), pp. 225-245.

[2]   Mark Whittle, *Cosmology: The History and Nature of Our Universe, Course Guidebook* (USA: The Teaching Company, 2008), pp. 129-133.

[3]   Mark Whittle, *Cosmology: The History and Nature of Our Universe, Course Guidebook* (USA: The Teaching Company, 2008), pp. 217-223. For all events during the first 5 BY.

[4]   Eduardo F. del Peloso, *et al.*, "The Age of the Galactic Thin Disk from Th/Eu Nucleocosmochronology: Extended Sample," *Proceedings of the International Astronomical Union* v.1 (23 December 2005) pp. 485-486 (Cambridge University Press).

[5]   Alfio Bonanno, Helmut Schlattl and Lucio Paternò, "The Age of the Sun and the Relativistic Corrections in the EOS," *A&A* 390/3 (2002), pp. 1115-1118.

[6]   (i) Mark Whittle, *Cosmology: The History and Nature of Our Universe, Course Guidebook* (USA: The Teaching Company, 2008), pp. 169-173.

(ii) Paul J. Steinhardt, "The Inflation Debate—Is the Theory at the Heart of Modern Cosmology Deeply Flawed?" *Scientific American*, April 2011, pp. 38-43.

[7]   Michael Marshall, "Timeline: The Evolution of Life," *New Scientist*, 14 July 2009.

[8]   Keith B. Miller, "The Precambrian to Cambrian Fossil Record and Transitional Forms," *PSCF* 49 (December 1997), pp. 264-268.

[9]   Stephen Jay Gould, "The Evolution of Life on Earth," *Scientific American*, October 1994, pp. 85-91.

[10]   Ibid. Examples of anatomical themes are: bilateral or radial symmetry, digestive system, nerve networks, internal or external skeletons, and major internal organs.

[11]   (i) Bowring, S.A., J.P. Grotzinger, C.E. Isachsen, A.H. Knoll, S.M. Pelechaty, and P. Kolosov, "Calibrating Rates of Early Cambrian Evolution," *Science* v.261, 1993, pp. 1293-1298.

(ii) Budd, G. E., Jensen, S. "A critical reappraisal of the fossil record of the bilaterian phyla". *Biological Reviews of the Cambridge Philosophical Society* v.75 (2), 2000, pp. 253–295.

[12]   (i) Michael Marshall, "Timeline: The Evolution of Life," *New Scientist*, 14 July 2009.

(ii) Stephen Jay Gould, *The Book of Life: An Illustrated History of the Evolution of Life on Earth*, Second Edition (New York: W. W. Norton Inc., 2001).

(iii) David M. Raup and J. John Sepkoski Jr., "Mass Extinctions in the Marine Fossil Record," *Science* v.215 No. 4539, 19 March 1982, pp.1501-1503.

(iv) John Alroy, "Dynamics of Origination and Extinction in the Marine Fossil Record," *The National Academy of Sciences of the USA*, 105 Supplement_1 (2008 August 12), pp.11536–11542.

Chapter 4

Interpreting the Scriptures

Many people read the Bible generally, and Genesis in particular, as a mythological account of human origins. Some take the Bible's account quite literally.

Is it possible that Genesis contains a reliable timeline for the development of the universe and the appearance of life on earth?

If so, how complete is that information, and how does it compare to today's scientific answers?

As we have seen in Chapter 1 of this book, Genesis is not intended to be a science text. However, given that it is part of the Torah, and the Torah provides a blueprint for creation, it must represent an accurate description of events and their timing. The whole creation account in Genesis Chapters 1 through 3 is only about 2,000 words (reproduced in Annex A for reference), shorter than most introductory chapters of cosmology or evolution books. Can it possibly contain a detailed timeline of such rich meaning in so few words? And where can we find the formula to convert the creation timeline to the time of events as measured by scientists (Human Time)?

Fortunately, the Torah consists of both the Written Law and the Oral Law. The brief account of our origins in the Written Law as detailed in Genesis is elaborated on significantly in the Oral Law. This oral tradition, together with related commentaries and mystical works, rivals, even when confined to the creation account only, the combined length of many contemporary cosmology and biology books. In fact, the Torah offers in-depth descriptions of what has happened since the beginning of time, as well as why and when. This constitutes the Genesis timeline for the development of the universe and the appearance of life on earth.

The purpose of this chapter is to briefly summarize the method used to extract information about creation events and their timing from Genesis, to examine the sources that help us do so, and to look at key characters behind some of these sources. This chapter is not an exhaustive review of this very complex subject; rather, it is designed to provide an abbreviated understanding of the sources used throughout the rest of the book to arrive at a comparison of the creation narrative with scientific theory and observation. It is also intended to inspire admiration for the richness of the biblical sources. This chapter is not a description of the biblical answer to the timeline for the development of the universe and the appearance of life on earth (unlike Chapter 3, which describes the science-based answer). The biblical answer is developed in later chapters, as required, in order to form a comparison with science's answer.

The rest of the book includes many references to biblical topics; these primarily are found in the sources described in Chapter 4.

Genesis as a Valuable Information Source

The biblical Hebrew language is unlike any other language. While its letters being pictographs is not unique, that each letter represents both letter and number does set it apart from other human communication systems. The numerical value of the letter, and therefore the word or sentence made from the letter, contains meaningful information that itself has become a focus of study regarding mystical aspects of the oral tradition as found in Kabbalah.

The shape of the letter contains deep significance and meaning and likewise conduces to a major field of study. Hebrew is written right to left. For example, the first letter of Genesis, ב, has three closed sides and an open left side. The first letter denotes the start of history that will be developed in progression to the left— the rest of the text. The immediate lesson to derive from this letter is that the world was created incomplete, i.e., with an open side.

The job of humankind is thus to complete creation by perfecting it. In fact, when the perfecting is complete, in the messianic age, the letter will be closed and become like a square "o." Elaborations on the meaning of the shape of this letter go on for pages in Kabbalistic literature.

Reading Hebrew text is akin to reading simultaneously English (i.e., letters and words), reading a scientific formula (e.g., chemical or physics formula), and reading an abstract diagram explaining various connections and processes. In addition to this richness within the text, there is the divinely revealed elaboration of the text in the oral tradition, providing even more detail, helping to guide interpretation, and connecting various sections of the Bible in order for one to glean even further information.

Needless to say, the process of reading the text to discern its full meaning requires years of study, an amazing memory and intellect, and teamwork. An effort not unlike developing a theory such as the Big Bang.

Let us now look at the process and sources used in this book to arrive at the Human Time events described in Genesis.

How Is Genesis Used to Derive Human Time for the Events That Scientists Have Measured?

Figure 4.1 on the following page illustrates the biblical sources and how they are used in the book.

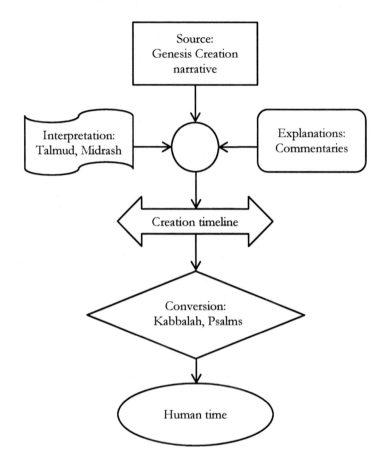

Figure 4.1 Biblical Sources

The process followed to arrive at Human Time for events in the Genesis narrative is as follows:

1. We begin with the fundamental source—the Genesis creation narrative.

2. We use the oral tradition to interpret Genesis to obtain a more exact time for each creation event and to organize events where the Genesis narrative is not chronological (e.g., Genesis Chapter 2).

3. We consult key commentaries (and in particular, two described later in this chapter) for clarification and explanations of terms, events, and meaning.

4. Having arrived at an understanding of the creation events and the time at which they happen (the creation timeline), we convert from Creation Time to Human Time using the mystical Kabbalistic works.

Let us now review the sources and characters in each of these steps. The fundamental source Genesis has been described already; at this point a review of Annex A containing the Genesis creation text maybe helpful.

Interpretation: The Oral Tradition

Two key components of the Oral Law provide more exact times for each creation event and help us to chronologically organize events: the Talmud and some Midrashim. These sources, along with the rest of the oral tradition, are thought to have been taught to Moses.[1] In fact, they are the reason why Moses remained so long on the mountain (as described in the Book of Exodus), as God could have given him the written law in one day. Moses is said to have transmitted this Oral Law to Joshua; Joshua, in turn, to the seventy Elders; the Elders to the Prophets; and the Prophets to the Great Synagogue.[2] It is believed the teachings were later transmitted successively to certain rabbis. Following the destruction of the Second Temple and the fall of Jerusalem in 70 CE, it became apparent that the Hebrew community and its learning resources were threatened, and further apparent that publication was the only way to ensure the law would be preserved. Thus, around 200 CE, a preserved version of the Oral Law in writing was completed.

The Talmud gets its name from the word *Lamud*, or taught, and meaning the Teaching. The Mishnah is the foundation and the principal part of the Talmud. It was expounded in the Academies in Babylon and in Israel during the Middle Ages. In this book, all Talmud references are from the Babylonian Talmud. As the interpretations increased with the passing of time, the disputations and decisions of the doctors of the law concerning the Mishnah were written down, and these writings constituted another part of the Talmud called the Gemarah. The Mishnah serves first as a kind of redaction of law, and is followed by the Gemarah serving as an analysis of its various opinions leading to definite decisions.

What kind of information does the Talmud reveal about timelines and creation? Below is an excerpt of the detailed timeline for the creation of man revealed for Day 6.

> *The day consisted of twelve hours. In the first hour, his [Adam's] dust was gathered; in the second, it was kneaded into a shapeless mass. In the third, his limbs were shaped; in the fourth...*[3]

Midrash means exposition and denotes the non-legalistic teachings of the Rabbis of the Talmudic era. Midrash[4] designates a critical explanation or analysis which, going more deeply than the mere literal sense, attempts to penetrate into the spirit of the scriptures, to examine the text from all sides, and thereby to derive interpretations that are not immediately obvious.

In the centuries following the compilation of the Talmud (around 505 CE), much of this material was compiled into collections known as Midrashim. A prominent example of a Midrash used throughout this book is the Midrash Rabbah, which adds critical details to the five books of Moses; another example is Pirkê de Rabbi Eliezer, which includes astronomical discussions related to the creation narrative.

Table 4.1 provides a summary timeline of events and personalities described in this chapter.

Table 4.1 Timeline of Biblical Sources and Personalities

Time—Biblical Year	Time—Western calendar	Event or person
1	3760 BCE	Adam & Eve created
2448	1313 BCE	Torah received by Moses
	1st - 2nd century	*Author of Pirkê de Rabbi Eliezer*
3979	219 CE	Mishna compiled
	3rd century	*Author of Midrash Rabbah*
4128	368 CE	Jerusalem Talmud compiled
4186	426 CE	Babylonian Talmud compiled
4260	500 CE	Babylonian Talmud recorded
4800 - 4865	1040 - 1105 CE	Rashi
4954 - 5030	1194-1270 CE	Ramban
	13th century	Zohar appears in Spain
	13-14th century	*Isaac ben Samuel of Acre*

Midrash Rabbah

Midrash Rabbah[5] is dedicated to explaining the five books of Moses. Genesis Rabbah is a Midrash to Genesis, assigned by tradition to the renowned Jewish scholar of Palestine, Hoshaiah (circa third century), who commented on the teachings of the Oral Law. The Midrash forms a commentary on the whole of Genesis. The biblical text is expounded verse for verse, often word for word; only genealogic passages and similar non-narrative information for exposition are omitted.

Midrash Rabbah contains many simple explanations of words and sentences, often in the Aramaic language, suitable for the instruction of youth; it also includes the most varied expositions popular in the public lectures of the synagogues and schools. According to the material or the sources at the disposal of the editor of the Midrash, he has strung together various longer or shorter explanations and interpretations of the successive passages, sometimes anonymously, sometimes citing the author. He adds to the running commentary connected in some way with the verse in question, or with one of its explanations—a method not unusual in the Talmud and in other Midrashim. The first chapters of Genesis, on the creation of the world and of humans, in turn furnish especially rich material for this type of commentary. Whole sections are devoted to discussion of one or two verses of Genesis.

What kind of information does Midrash Rabbah reveal about timelines and creation? For example, it tells us[6] that Adam and Eve sinned exactly three hours before sundown on Day 6. This level of detail is essential in establishing the age of the universe and dating the appearance of life on earth.

Pirkê de Rabbi Eliezer

Pirkê de Rabbi Eliezer (or "Chapters of Rabbi Eliezer")[7] comprises ethical guidelines as well as astronomical discussions related to the Creation narrative. Much information that is not found in other sources is revealed in this work.

Despite the book's bearing an author's name, the actual writer is unknown. The reputed author is Rabbi Eliezer, who lived in the latter half of the first century CE and in the first decades of the second century. He was famous for his great scholarship and is quoted in the Mishnah and Talmud more frequently than any of his contemporaries. Did this owe to the very fact that the actual writer of Chapters of Rabbi Eliezer deliberately selected the name of this famous master in Israel as its supposed author? In many respects the book is controversial and unorthodox—controversial in opposing doctrines and traditions current in certain circles of former times; unorthodox in revealing certain mysteries (including creation mysteries) that were reputed to have been taught in the school of Rabban Jochanan ben Zakkai, the teacher of Rabbi Eliezer.

Who exactly was the teacher of Rabbi Eliezer? Rabban Jochanan ben Zakkai,[8] who flourished in the first century CE, helped to preserve and develop Judaism in the years following the destruction of the Second Temple of Jerusalem in 70 CE. He is said to have been smuggled out of the besieged city in a coffin and to have visited the Roman camp and persuaded the future emperor Vespasian to allow him to set up an academy at Jabneh near the Judaean coast. He established an authoritative rabbinic body there and was revered as a great teacher and scholar. According to the Mishnah,[9] traditions were handed down through an unbroken chain of scholars; Jochanan, in receiving the teachings of Hillel and Shammai, formed the last link in that chain. Before his death, Hillel is said to have prophetically designated Johanan, his youngest pupil, as "the father of wisdom" and "the father of coming generations."

What did Rabbi Eliezer learn about creation? For example, one key detail is that the sun is older than the moon by a period of less than 2/3 of an hour (in Creation Time).[10]

Explanations—The Commentaries

Commentaries are critical explanations or interpretations of the biblical texts. The process of arriving at these explanations is rigorous and involves very specific and well-developed rules and methods for the investigation and exact determination of the meaning of the Scriptures, both legal and historical.

The interpretation of the text examines its extended meaning. As a general rule, the extended meaning never contradicts the base meaning. Commentaries work at four levels of meaning: (1) the plain or contextual meaning of the text, (2) the allegorical meaning or symbolic meaning beyond just the literal sense, (3) the metaphorical meaning or comparative meaning as derived from other similar occurrences in the text, and (4) the hidden meaning or the mystical meaning. There is often considerable overlap, for example, when legal understandings of a verse are influenced by mystical interpretations, or when a hint is determined by comparing a word with other instances of the same word.

Two major commentaries used throughout this book are those by Rashi and Ramban. Rashi's commentary is widely known for presenting the plain meaning of the text in a concise yet lucid fashion. Ramban's commentary attempts to discover the hidden meanings of scriptural words.

Rashi

Shlomo Yitzhaki (1040–1105 CE), better known by the acronym Rashi[11] (RAbbi SHlomo Itzhaki), was a medieval French Rabbi famed as the author of the first comprehensive commentary on the Talmud, as well as a comprehensive commentary on the Written Law (including Genesis). His is considered the father of all commentaries that followed on the Talmud and the Written Law.

Acclaimed for his ability to present the basic meaning of the text succinctly, Rashi appeals to both learned scholars and beginning students, and his works remain a centerpiece of contemporary study. His commentary on the Talmud, which covers nearly all of the Babylonian Talmud, has been included in every edition of the Talmud since its first printing in the 1520s. His commentary on the Five Books of Moses is an indispensable aid to students of all levels. The latter commentary alone serves as the basis for more than three hundred super-commentaries that analyze Rashi's choice of language and citations.

Rashi began to write his famous commentary at an early age. The Torah was very difficult to understand properly, and the Talmud was even more difficult. Rashi decided to write a commentary in simple language that would make it easy for everyone to learn and understand the Torah. But Rashi was modest, and even after he had become famous far and wide, he hesitated to come out into the open with his commentary. He wanted to make sure that it would be favorably received. So he wrote his commentaries on slips of parchment and set out on a two years' journey, visiting the various Torah academies of those days. He went incognito, hiding his identity.

Rashi came to a Torah academy and sat down to listen to the lecture of the attending Rabbi. There came a difficult passage that the Rabbi struggled to explain to his students. When Rashi was left alone, he took the slip with his commentary, in which that passage was explained simply and clearly, and put it into one of the Rabbi's books. On the following morning when the Rabbi opened his book, he found a mysterious slip of parchment in which the passage was so clearly and simply explained that he was amazed. He told his students about it. Rashi listened to their praises of his commentary and saw how useful it was to the students, but he did not say that it was his. And so Rashi went on visiting various academies of the Torah in many cities, and everywhere he planted his slips of commentaries secretly. The way these slips were received made Rashi realize more and more how needed they were, and he continued to write his commentaries. Finally, Rashi was discovered planting his commentary in the usual manner, and the secret was out.

What kind of information on the Creation narrative does Rashi reveal? For example, he teaches that when the Genesis text says *"it was good,"* this indicates that what was made was completed to the point that it was useful to humans, and had therefore attained its intended state.[12]

Ramban

Nahmanides, also known as Rabbi Moses ben Nachman Girondi, Bonastrucça Porta, and by his acronym Ramban[13] (Gerona, 1194–Land of Israel, 1270), was a leading medieval scholar, Rabbi, philosopher, physician, Kabbalist, and biblical commentator. His commentary on the five books of Moses was his last work and his best known. He is considered one of the Elder Sages of mystical Judaism, who are known to have been experts in Kabbalah. The Ramban's commentary on the Torah is considered to be based on Kabbalistic knowledge, careful scholarship, and original study of the Bible.

Ramban showed great talent at a very early age. He was a brilliant student, and his scholarship, piety, and very fine character made him famous far beyond his own community. At the age of sixteen he had mastered the whole Talmud with all its commentaries. Nahmanides also studied medicine and philosophy. Not wishing to profit from the Torah, Ramban became a practicing physician in his native town. However, at the same time he was the communal Rabbi of Gerona, and later became the chief Rabbi of the entire province of Catalonia in Spain.

What kind of information pertaining to the story of creation does Ramban reveal? Frankly, astounding information. For example, his description of the development of the universe bears an uncanny resemblance to Big Bang descriptions found in today's physics books:

> At the briefest instant following creation all the matter of the universe was concentrated in a very small place, no larger than a grain of mustard. The matter at this time was very thin, so intangible, that it did not have real substance. It did have, however, a potential to gain substance and form and to become tangible matter. From the initial concentration of this intangible substance in its minute location, the substance expanded, expanding the

universe as it did so. As the expansion progressed, a change in the substance occurred. This initially thin noncorporeal substance took on the tangible aspects of matter as we know it. From this initial act of creation, from this ethereally thin pseudosubstance, everything that has existed, or will ever exist, was, is, and will be formed.[14]

This was written about 800 years ago.

Time Conversion—Mystical Works

The works described so far (along with a few more) are used towards developing an accurate biblical representation of the creation timeline. To convert from Creation Time to Human Time, the mystical Kabbalistic sources are required.

Kabbalah is the ancient Jewish mystical tradition that teaches the deepest insights into the essence of God, His interaction with the world, and the purpose of Creation. The Kabbalah and its teachings—no less than the Law—are an integral part of the oral tradition. They are traced back to the revelation to Moses at Sinai, and some even before (one book is said to have been Adam's). The Kabbalah teaches[15] that science will inform spirituality, and spirituality will inform science by the time the Messianic era arrives. Kabbalah means reception, for we cannot physically perceive the Divine; we merely study the mystical truths.

The primary Kabbalistic work is the Zohar.[16] The work is a revelation from God communicated through R. Shimon bar Yochai to the latter's select disciples. Under the form of a commentary on the five books of Moses, written partly in Aramaic and partly in Hebrew, it contains a complete Kabbalistic theosophy discussing the nature of God, the cosmogony and cosmology of the universe, the soul, sin, redemption, good, evil, and so on.

The Zohar first appeared in Spain in the 13th century and was published by Moses de Leon. De Leon ascribed the work to

Shimon bar Yochai, a Rabbi of the second century, who, during the Roman persecution, hid in a cave for thirteen years studying the Torah and was divinely inspired to write the Zohar.

There are many Kabbalistic works, some more mainstream than others. To convert timelines we rely primarily on *Otzar Ha-Chaim*, the Kabbalistic work of Isaac ben Samuel of Acre.

Isaac ben Samuel of Acre

Isaac ben Samuel of Acre[17] (fl. 13th–14th centuries) was a Kabbalist who lived in the Land of Israel. It is thought Isaac ben Samuel was a pupil of Ramban. Isaac ben Samuel was at Acre when that town was taken by Al-Malik al-Ashraf, and he was thrown into prison with many of his fellow believers. Escaping the massacre, in 1305 he went to Spain. This was the time that Moses de Leon discovered the Zohar.

According to Azulai,[18] Isaac of Acre is frequently quoted by prominent Kabbalists (e.g., R. Hayyim Vital; Calabria, 1543–Damascus, 1620). He was an expert in composing the sacred names of God, by the power of which angels were forced to reveal to him the great mysteries. He wrote many Kabbalistic works.

R. Isaac developed an original methodology of interpretation, which he designated as the "four ways of NiSAN," being the acronym of Nistar (hidden), Sod (secret), Emet (truth), and Emet Nekhona (correct truth). The four ways of NiSAN are used by R. Isaac only in his later works, including *Otzar HaChaim*. This work was translated to English recently by Rabbi Kaplan, described in his own words as follows:[19]

> There is only one complete copy of this manuscript in the world, and this is in the Guenzberg Collection in the Lenin Library in Moscow.... This is how I got my hands on this very rare and important manuscript.... It took a while to decipher the handwriting, since it is an ancient script.

What did Rabbi Kaplan discover when he translated the text? He found a method for converting Creation Time to Human Time. He also found that R. Isaac, in his work *Otzar HaChaim*, was the first to imply that the universe is billions of years old—at a time when the prevalent thought was that the universe was thousands of years old. Isaac arrived at this conclusion by distinguishing between earthly "solar years" and "divine years," herein described as Human Time and Divine Time.

Moving through the steps illustrated in Figure 4.1, we discover the timing of creation events, applying the work of R. Isaac, with some refinements. We can then convert the time of these events to Human Time.

The next chapter develops the time conversion process in detail.

---

1   Yerushalami Peah 6:2.

2   Rabbi Moshe Lieber, *Ethics of our Fathers* (New York, Mesorah Publications Ltd, 2003), Chapter 1:1.

3   Babylonian Talmud, Sanhedrin 38b.

4   Joseph Jacobs, S. Horovitz, Midrah, 2002, JewishEncyclopedia.com.

5   Marcus Jastrow, J. Theodor, Bereshit Rabbah, 2002, Jewish Encyclopedia.com.

6   Exodus Midrash Rabbah 32:1.

7   Michael Friedlander, *Pirkê de Rabbi Eliezer* [part of the oral law]. (Illinois: Varda Books, 2004), Introduction.

8   Solomon Schechter and Wilhelm Bacher, Johanan b. Zakkai, 2002, JewishEncyclopedia.com.

9   Mishnah (Ab. ii. 8).

[10]   Michael Friedlander, *Pirkê de Rabbi Eliezer* [part of the oral law]. (Illinois: Varda Books, 2004), Chapter 7.

[11]   Joseph Jacobs, Morris Liber, M. Seligsohn, Rashi, 2002, JewishEncyclopedia.com.

[12]   Rashi's commentary on Genesis 1:4.

[13]   Nissan Mindel, *Talks and Tales* (New York: Merkos L'inyonei Chinuch, 2003).

[14]   Ramban on Genesis 1:1, quoted in Gerald Schroeder, *Genesis and the Big Bang: The Discovery of Harmony Between Modern Science and the Bible* (New York, Bantam Books, 1990), p. 65.

[15]   Zohar I, 117a.

[16]   Joseph Jacobs, Isaac Broydé, Zohar, 2002, JewishEncyclopedia.com.

[17]   (i) Kaufmann Kohler, M. Seligsohn, Isaac ben Samuel of Acre, 2002, JewishEncyclopedia.com.

(ii) Rabbi Aryeh Kaplan, *The Age of the Universe: A Torah True Perspective* (Rueven Meir Caplan, 2008).

[18]   Chaim Joseph David ben Isaac Zerachia Azulai (1724–21 March 1807) was a rabbinical scholar who pioneered the history of Jewish religious writings.

[19]   Rabbi Aryeh Kaplan, *The Age of the Universe: A Torah True Perspective* (Rueven Meir Caplan, 2008).

Chapter 5

Conversion of Times

I shall take you out from under the burdens of Egypt... I shall re-deem you with an outstretched arm and with great judgments.[1]

An outstretched arm? Is it possible that God has a tangible arm?

A fundamental belief of those who accept the Bible's teachings is that God does not have a material body.[2] Yet the Bible is full of allusions to God in human terms: his hand, his breath, his arm. Maimonides, an eminent Jewish philosopher and one of the greatest Torah scholars of the Middle Ages, includes God not having a material body as one of the thirteen principles of faith[3] (in his Commentary on the Mishnah). He further explains: "The Torah speaks in the language of men." Does the Torah speak in analogies?

It does not.

Every word in the Torah is real and carries deep meaning. God's arm is really an arm. But what does God's arm mean? We simply don't know. Can we gain some insight, hint, or understanding of what God's arm means by looking at our own arm as the analogy? By all means.

The Torah is real—our world is the analogy.

To extend the reasoning, what does a biblical creation day mean? An earth day is the result of the earth spinning on its axis, making the sun appear to rise, move across the sky, set, and do so again every 24 hours. For astronauts on board the space station, a day (from sunrise to sunrise) is approximately 90 minutes. On the planet Venus a day is 243 earth days—so very different from a day on earth, and yet still called a day.

Yet, "The Torah speaks in the language of men."

A creation day is something extraordinary, perhaps 2.5 billion years in length. Our earth day is simply an analogy to help us understand what is meant by a creation day.

A computer has an internal clock that runs very fast. In fact, every six months or so we want to buy a new computer partly because the new one has a faster clock—1 GHz, 2 GHz.... Yet, when we look at the computer screen or when the computer logs the time of our e-mails, it uses time we understand, therefore relying on two different clocks: one to drive the inner workings of the computer, and another to communicate with us.

Creation Time is used by God to communicate with us—something we can relate to, comprehend, remember, and explain to children. But this is not the time by which the universe operates.

God is above time; past, present, and future are all one to him.[4] Yet, the action of creation requires God to contract his infinity and create a clock—a divine clock to keep Divine Time by which the universe operates.

Here on earth, in the midst of physical creation, there is another clock—one for keeping Human Time—as measured by our heartbeat, the sun's shadow, the swing of the pendulum.

Thus, we can now understand the differences among three distinct time measurements:

1. Creation Time is used by God to communicate with us, with its meaning hidden by the human language in which it is expressed, or creation days.

2. Divine Time is the actual time on which the universe operates.

3. Human Time is the time measured by our earthly clocks.

Today, the only measurement we rely upon is Human Time. We observe the universe and record those observations using our clocks. Yet before Adam sinned, when God was observing events, he used Divine Time—a special clock invented for this purpose. Nonetheless, He told us the creation story "in the language of men" using the words creation days (i.e., in Creation Time).

This chapter describes all three types of time (Creation, Divine, and Human) and explores the timelines of each to show how we can convert from one type of time to another. The remainder of the book will then use the conversion factors derived in this chapter to convert the Creation Time of events in the Genesis narrative to Human Time (as measured by scientists), allowing us to compare the creation account to scientific theories and observations.

SECTION 1—CREATION TIME

"The Torah speaks in the language of men."

In this section we first examine the meaning of "language of men" key terms and concepts so that we can understand the timeline described in the first three chapters of Genesis.

We then look at Day 6 to understand the creation timeline. The focus of this section is on the overall structure of the creation timeline and the details of the hour-by-hour events of Day 6 as they pertain to man.

The rest of the creation timeline, including more detail for Day 6 and Days 1 to 5, will be developed when a comparison is made to science-derived times for the same events in subsequent chapters.

Key Concepts

Creation (God Created) vs. Formation (God Said Let, or Separate, or Bring Forth or...)

Not all so-called acts of creation are equal.

Genesis uses two distinct words to describe God's actions in the Genesis account: creation and formation. Creation is the divine act of making something out of nothing (such as a magician seemingly pulling a handkerchief out of thin air). Formation refers to taking something that already exists and making it into something else (e.g., building a table from wood).

There are only three acts of creation mentioned in Genesis: (1) the creation of the initial material of the universe at the beginning of the first day, (2) the creation of sea creatures on Day 5, and (3) the creation of humankind's spiritual part, meaning the provision of a Godly soul (the body is formed from dust). Everything else described in the account of creation is an act of formation.

A Two-Step Process[5]

Important creations and formations are accomplished in two operations.

The first operation, to bring forth or to endow, means to invest something with a capability.

The second operation is the actual formation (or creation) of a physical entity. For example, in the case of plants, the earth is first invested with the power to grow, or give life to, any seeds sown on it. The second operation is to form the actual physical vegetation. The earth is then able to grow vegetation on its surface.

In Day 3 the text says, "*Let the earth sprout vegetation...*"[6] i.e., "*Let it endow itself with the power to sprout grass.*"[7]

In Day 6 the text says, "*And all the herb of the field had not yet sprouted, for God had not sent rain upon the earth and there was no man to work the soil.*"[8] That is to say, it is clear there is no vegetation until Day 6—when, and only then, after man is completed, does it physically appear on earth.[9]

The same process can be seen with respect to other creations, for instance, animals. Furthermore, in some cases there is a third step. The third step occurs when what has been formed or created is told to replicate itself, i.e., to *"be fruitful and multiply."* It is after this command that one expects to find fossil evidence of what has been formed or created.

The Working Day

The day in the Genesis text is described as a 24-hour period from evening to sunset. We learn from the details about Day 6 (described in the Talmud[10] and reproduced below in the creation timeline section) that God works at making physical items for a period of 12 hours. Furthermore, since the work for Day 6 is finished at sunset, he must work the second 12 hours of the day, i.e., the daylight hours.

By extension we deduce that the main work in Days 1 through 5 is also done during the second 12 hours of the day. This assumption is reinforced by the general concept that God follows his own Torah, where the labor laws also specify that the norm is to work during the 12 daylight hours (although work at night is allowed). The Talmud provides the employment rules for workers where no other arrangement has been made; workers are to leave the house at sunrise, go to work, work until sunset, and return in their own time after sunset.[11]

We also learn from the Talmud text provided for Day 6 that whatever appears as the first act of the day happens exactly at the beginning of the working day—sunrise, and the last thing to be discussed happens at the very end of the day—nightfall.

Godly Attributes

Sefirah (plural: sefirot)[12] is a channel of divine energy or life force. A fundamental concept of Kabbalah is that in the process of creation, an intermediate stage emanated from God's infinite light to create what we experience as human existence. These intermediate stage channels are called variously the Ten Sefirot, Ten Divine Emanations, or Ten Divine Powers.

In the subsequent sixteenth century transcendent Kabbalistic scheme of Isaac Luria (thus, the Lurianic Kabbalah), the Sefirot are categorized as shown in Table 5.1 below.

Table 5.1 The Ten Sefirot

Category	Sefirah
Conscious intellect	1 Wisdom 2 Understanding 3 Knowledge
Conscious emotions	(Primary emotions) 4 Kindness 5 Severity 6 Beauty
	(Secondary emotions) 7 Eternity 8 Glory 9 Foundation
	(Vessel to bring action) 10 Kingship

It is via the ten sefirot that God interacts with creation; they may thus be considered His attributes. The pattern of sefirot exists on many levels. Every object and every process in the world is working through the ten sefirot. Thus the ten sefirot are apparent in all reality: from the ten fingers to the ten parts of the soul, to all other aspects of physical creation.

In particular, the sefirot relate to the chemical elements and biological classifications of life. We will make use of this relation later to understand key aspects of the creation account. The two sefirot we will need to understand for this purpose are wisdom and kindness.

In the soul, wisdom is associated with the power of intuitive insight, which flashes, lightning-like, across consciousness on occasion. Wisdom also implies the ability to look deeply at some aspect of reality and abstract its conceptual essence to uncover its underlying truth. Wisdom is considered the primary (first) force in the creative process of the universe, as it is said: *"You have made them all with wisdom."*[13] The first words of Genesis, *"In the beginning of God's creating the heavens and the earth"* is translated into Aramaic as *"With wisdom [God created...]."*

The sefirah of kindness is the first of the emotive attributes of the sefirot. It is the desire to give without limitation. Kindness is also known as mercy. Rashi[14] examines the Hebrew text starting in Genesis 2.4[15] and explains that the inhabitants of the earth were created with the Godly attribute of mercy. Kabbalah explains that kindness was, in fact, the reason for the Creation. Since God's nature is absolute benevolence and loving kindness, He created life in order to bestow his kindness.[16]

Adam vs. Humankind

Adam, known as the first created man, is pictured by most as a man like others today. However, this is not the case. Adam was nothing like us physically or spiritually. Only after the sin was he greatly diminished and so became closer to what we imagine; before the sin he was substantially different.

The Talmud provides physical descriptions of Adam that include a cosmic being: *"Adam extended from the earth to the firmament... from one end of the earth to the other,"*[17] a body made of light and a mind that could comprehend the universe.[18]

Adam would have been eternal if he had not committed the sin of disobedience. The Midrash teaches that Adam was so different from us today that the very angels thought he was a deity: *"When he was created the angels erred (thinking he was a divine being) and wished to sing 'Holy' before him."* [19]

As we will see below, the creation timeline shows that Adam (and Eve) was alive for much of Day 6 (hundreds of millions of years ago). However, this does not mean there was a human, as we know it today, alive at that time. Humanity as we know it came much later, around the time of the sin (thousands of years ago). The language employed in this book from this point forward uses the term Adam and man interchangeably (representing a special being). The term humankind is used to denote our species.

The Creation Timeline

The creation timeline comprises the six days of creation, each broken into 24 hours, with (as we have seen above) God's work occurring throughout the second 12-hour period of each day. This six-day period is subsequently followed by 6,000 years of history, followed by the 1,000 years of the seventh millennium,[20] thereby completing the full biblical timeline. To illustrate the timeline, we examine Day 6.

Adam (and humankind that descended from him) is the most important creation—everything is made for him and his kind. Thus, the Talmud provides a detailed account of man and his actions during Day 6, hour by hour.

> The day consisted of twelve hours. In the first hour, his [Adam's] dust was gathered; in the second, it was kneaded into a shapeless mass. In the third, his limbs were shaped; in the fourth, a soul was infused into him; in the fifth, he arose and stood on his feet; in the sixth, he gave [the animals] their names; in the seventh, Eve became his mate; in the eighth, they ascended to bed as two and descended as four [i.e., Cain and Abel were born—ed.]; in the ninth, he was commanded not to eat of the tree; in the tenth, he sinned; in the eleventh, he was tried; and in the twelfth he was expelled [from Eden] and departed, for it is written, Man abideth not in honor.[21]

Figure 5.1 illustrates Day 6, which is shown as having one 12-hour period of darkness (shaded) followed by twelve individual daylight hours. The numbers signify the hour of the day: 1 is the first hour (typically 6 a.m. to 7 a.m.).

Details for other Creation days will be examined in later chapters.

Creation Time	Creation Events
12	
1	Dust was gathered
2	Dust kneaded into shapeless mass; Formation of complex life begins
3	Adam's limbs shaped
4	Soul infused into Adam
5	Adam rose and stood on his feet
6	Adam named the animals
7	Eve was created
8	Cain and Abel born. Garden is planted after man created
9	Adam and Eve are commanded not to eat from the Tree
10	Adam and Eve sinned
11	Adam and Eve were tried
12	Adam and Eve were expelled from the Garden

(Rows 1–12 of Creation Time fall under the heading DAY 6 (hours))

Figure 5.1 Creation Time—Day 6

SECTION 2—DIVINE TIME

Divine Time is the fundamental inner working clock of the universe.

Divine Time is explained in detail in Annex B where it is shown that one Creation Day is equivalent to 7,000 Divine Years.

SECTION 3—HUMAN TIME

Human Time is measured with clocks and instruments. In this section we explore its relation to Divine Time and to Creation Time.

The Human Timeline

What time do humans measure when probing the cosmos with space telescopes or when dating fossil records?

When God is considered the conscious observer, we must necessarily convert Divine Time to time as experienced by humans (Human Time). The conversion factor is provided for us in Psalms as interpreted in the Talmud: one divine day is 1,000 years of Human Time.[22] As illustrated in Table 5.2, given that a calendar year is 365.25 days (a leap year with one extra day occurs every four years, thus on average each year is 365 and one-quarter days), then one divine year equates to 365,250 years of Human Time.

Thus, in order to obtain Human Time from Divine Time, we multiply Divine Time by 365,250. Creation Time is converted to Human Time by multiplying it by 7,000 (conversion of Creation Time to Divine Time) and again by 365,250 (conversion of Divine Time to Human Time). One Creation day is therefore equal to 2.56 BY of Human Time (see Table 5.2). The time conversion formula is very simple:

1 Creation Day= 7000 x 1000 x 365.25 = 2.56 billion years

Once man becomes the conscious observer, the conversion factor becomes one, e.g., one year is one year, and one hour is one hour.

Table 5.2 Human Time vs. Creation Time

Year	365.25 days	
Divine Day	1,000 years in Human Time	
Divine Year	365,250 years in Human Time	= 356.25 x 1000
Creation Day	7,000 Divine Years	
Creation Day	2.56 billion years in Human Time	= 365,250 x 7000
Creation hour	106.53 million years in Human Time	= 2.56 BY ÷ 24
Creation second	29,592 years in Human Time	= 106.53 MY ÷ 3600
Creation Day	0.934×10^{12} days in Human Time	= 2.56 BY x 365.25

Historically, authors[23] have applied a conversion factor from Creation Time to Human Time to the cycles prior to Adam. Here we cannot apply the conversion factor directly to the 7,000 year cycles within each of the six creation days for two reasons: (1) the start time of physical creation is not the beginning of Day 1, and (2) the point in time when God ceases to be the conscious observer does not occur at the end of Day 6. This section explores the start and end times for the conversion from Creation Time to Human Time.

The Start Time

Clearly, God is the conscious observer when creation of the universe starts. However, the physical creation starts on the sunrise of Day 1, or 12 hours into the day (refer to the section titled *The Working Day* under Key Concepts above). Before this time, nothing physical exists. When we now peer into our telescopes and develop the theory of the Big Bang, we extrapolate back in time to the point just before the density of the universe goes to infinity, and its size to zero. This *"in the beginning..."* occurs at precisely 12 hours into Day 1. As such, when we convert Creation Time to Human Time, we start with the first hour of daylight, or in Divine Time, the year 3,500 (7,000 years per day).

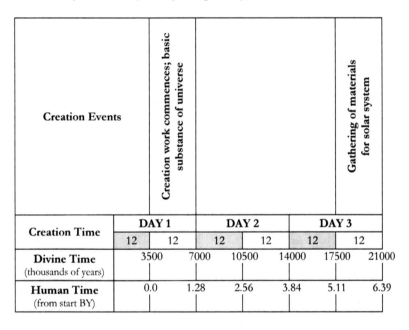

Creation Events	Creation work commences; basic substance of universe				Gathering of materials for solar system	
Creation Time	**DAY 1**		**DAY 2**		**DAY 3**	
	12	12	12	12	12	12
Divine Time (thousands of years)	3500	7000	10500	14000	17500	21000
Human Time (from start BY)	0.0	1.28	2.56	3.84	5.11	6.39

Figure 5.2 The First Three Days of Creation

Figure 5.2 shows the creation, divine, and human timelines for the first three days. Here the days are shown as two 12-hour periods (with the 12 hours of nighttime shaded). Human Time starts at zero halfway through Day 1 and progresses at approximately 1.28 BY per each 12-hour Creation Time period.

The End Time

The conversion from Creation Time to Human Time ends when man becomes the conscious observer.

When does man become the conscious observer? Is it at the end of Day 6, or when man is created, or perhaps some other time?

Prior work[24] has assumed it occurs when Adam is created. When man is first created, he is clearly at one with his Creator. In fact, he is still a composite male and female man, according to the Midrash.[25] Once he is judged and evicted from the Garden of Eden, he is clearly a separate conscious observer of his world.

The transition occurs when Adam sins. It is at this point that Adam separates from his Creator and makes a moral choice of his own. The biblical text is clear on this point:[26] *"Man has become like the unique One among us, knowing good and bad..."* Rashi elaborates: "unique one among us meaning that he has become unique among the terrestrial ones, just as God is unique among the celestial ones."

In the Talmud we are told that Adam sins during the tenth hour of the day.[27] However, Midrash Rabbah[28] makes it clear that Adam and Eve had to wait a mere three hours to inherit the blessing of Eden for all time; the sin occurred at the very beginning of the tenth hour.

After the tenth hour, time is as we experience it now, and less than 6,000 years have elapsed.

We are now ready to convert from Creation Time to Human Time and reveal what Genesis says about the timelines for the formation of the universe and for the development of life on earth.

---

[1]   Exodus 6:6.

[2] From translation of the full text of the thirteen foundations of Jewish belief compiled by Rabbi Moshe ben Maimon; Third Foundation.

[3] Ibid.

[4] Eliezer Zeiger, "Time, Space and Consciousness." BOr HaTorah Vol. 15, ed. Prof. Herman Branover (Israel: SHAMIR, 2005).

[5] H. Moose, *In the Beginning: The Bible Unauthorized* (California: Thirty Seven Books, 2001), pp. 96-97.

[6] Genesis 1:11.

[7] H. Moose, *In the Beginning: The Bible Unauthorized* (California: Thirty Seven Books, 2001), pp. 96-97. For a more complete explanation of what power to grow grass means, see Chapter 8, Land Plants.

[8] Genesis 2:5.

[9] H. Moose, *In the Beginning: The Bible Unauthorized* (California: Thirty Seven Books, 2001), p. 159.

[10] Babylonian Talmud, Sanhedrin 38b.

[11] Babylonian Talmud, Baba-Mezi'a, Chapters 6 and 7.

[12] Y David Schulman, *The Sefirot: Ten Emanations of Divine Power* (London: Jason Aronson Inc., 1996), Introduction.

[13] Psalm 104:24.

[14] Rashi on Genesis 2:4.

[15] Genesis is where Day 6 details are provided. See Annex A, starting with Genesis 2:4. The text no longer refers to God; instead it refers to the Lord God, in the KJV translation.

[16] This is derived from Psalms 89:3.

[17]   Babylonian Talmud, Chagigah 12a.

[18]   Howard Schwartz, *Tree of Souls: The Mythology of Judaism* (Oxford University Press, 2004), p.130.

[19]   Midrash, Rabbi Meir Zlotowitz, Bereishis, *Genesis / A New Translation with a Commentary Anthologized from Talmudic Midrashic and Rabbinic Sources* (New York: Mesorah Publications Ltd., 1977), p.13.

[20]   Zohar VaYera 119a, Ramban on Genesis 2:3 maintain that the seven days of creation correspond to seven millennia of the existence of natural creation. The tradition teaches that the seventh day of the week, Shabbat or the day of rest, corresponds to the Great Shabbat, the seventh millennium (years 6,000–7,000), the age of universal rest.

[21]   Babylonian Talmud, Sanhedrin 38b.

[22]   *"For a thousand years in your sight are but like yesterday when it is past"* (Psalm 90:4), as interpreted in the Babylonian Talmud, Sanhedrin 97a and 97b.

[23]   (i) Avi Rabinowitz and Herman Branover, "The Role of the Observer in Halakhah and Quantum Physics," H. Branover and I. Attia. eds. (Northvale, NJ: *Science in the Light of the Torah: A B'or Ha'Torah Reader*, 1994).

(ii) Rabbi Aryeh Kaplan, *The Age of the Universe: A Torah True Perspective* (Rueven Meir Caplan, 2008).

(iii) Alexander Poltorak, "On the Age of the Universe," BOr HaTorah Vol. 13, ed. Prof. Herman Branover (Israel: SHAMIR, 1999).

[24]   Ibid.

(iv) Alexander Poltorak, "The Age of the Universe Using the Many-Worlds Interpretation," BOr HaTorah Vol. 18, ed. Prof. Herman Branover (Israel: SHAMIR, 2008).

[25] Midrash, Rabbi Meir Zlotowitz, Bereishis, *Genesis / A New Translation with a Commentary Anthologized from Talmudic Midrashic and Rabbinic Sources* (New York: Mesorah Publications Ltd., 1977), p.72 on Genesis 1:27.

[26] Genesis 3:22 and commentary.

[27] Babylonian Talmud, Sanhedrin 38b.

[28] Exodus Midrash Rabbah 32:1.

Chapter 6

The Age of the Universe

So, how old is the universe?

Although there have been attempts to find a parallel meaning between the 13.7 BY scientific estimate and the 6,000-year literal biblical interpretation, there has been no precise biblically based calculation leading to exactly the same answer as produced by scientists.

How much time has elapsed from the Genesis statement "*In the beginning...*" or in scientific terms, from the Big Bang until now?

When it comes to the universe we have two distinct periods of counting time, which, as explained in Chapter 5, are recorded by different observers. While God is the conscious observer, the counting is done in Creation Time. When humankind takes charge as the conscious observer, the counting switches to Human Time.

Chapter 5 explains that the universe begins at sunrise of Day 1, or 12 hours into the day (remember, biblical day starts at nightfall, in the evening). The universe's development continues under God's conscious observation through all of Days 2, 3, 4, 5 and in Day 6 until three hours before the end of Day 6 (i.e., until the time of Adam's sin). Thus, the total time period of God as conscious observer is 5.375 creation days (1/2 of Day 1, full days on Days 2, 3, 4, and 5, and $21/24^{th}$ of a day on Day 6).

Late in Day 6 humankind takes over as the conscious observer and the counting of time. A total of 5,773 years have elapsed since that moment. The age of the universe is thus 5.375 creation days plus 5,773 human years.

In Chapter 5 we derived the conversion factor from Creation Time (in days) to Human Time (in years). Each creation day converts to 7,000 divine years, and each divine year converts to

365,250 human years. Multiplying the 5.375 creation day period by 7,000 and 365,250 yields a total of 13,743,000,000 (or 13.743 BY) in Human Time. We now add 5,773 years, an inconsequential amount of time compared to billions of years, to obtain the age of the universe.

Thus, according to Genesis, the universe is 13.743 BY old.

How old do scientists say the universe is?

We concluded in Chapter 3 that once the parameters that define the properties of the universe (i.e., the cosmological parameters) are established, the Big Bang theory produces an accurate and detailed timeline of the development of the universe. In particular, the theory can be used to calculate how much time has elapsed from the beginning until now—the age of the universe. To determine the cosmological parameters and crucially the best-fitting set of parameters, much scientific data about our universe must be gathered.

In recent years, two amazing instruments have allowed us to look deep into the universe and back in history toward the origins of the universe. These instruments are the Wilkinson Microwave Anisotropy Probe (WMAP) and the Hubble Space Telescope (HST).

The WMAP is a NASA earth-orbiting satellite that measures differences in the temperature of radiation left over from an early stage in the development of the universe—the Cosmic Microwave Background Radiation. WMAP was launched in 2001 and has recently completed its mission, producing some of the most up-to-date and accurate cosmological parameters towards calibrating the Big Bang theory.

The HST is also a NASA satellite. It carries a large, optically superb telescope above the earth's atmosphere (which distorts images obtained by earthbound telescopes), allowing for deep, clear views of the cosmos. Launched in 1990, the device has produced countless images ranging from our own solar system to the edge of the observable universe. It has recently also been used to determine certain cosmological parameters.

After years of cosmological observation and instrument data analysis, what age for the universe has been determined?

According to scientists, the universe is 13.75± 0.13 BY[1] old.

In scientific notation the symbol ± denotes that the number to the left can be higher or lower by the number on the right of the sign. Thus, 13.75 ± 0.13 means a number in the range of 13.62 to 13.88.

Prior Calculations of the Age of the Universe

Rabbi Kaplan[2] calculates the age of the universe to be 15,340,500,000 years, based on six cosmic cycles occurring prior to Adam. Since then, others have reworked this calculation and elaborated on it in more detail from a physics point of view.[3] However, they have continued to use six prior full cycles and thus obtain an age for the universe of over 15 BY.

Dr. Gerald Schroeder[4] utilizes a different method. Instead of reaching into the scriptures for a conversion factor from Creation Time to Human Time, he reaches into science for the conversion factor. He reasons that, since the universe is expanding, events in the past that were separated by a day are now separated by a much longer period. He uses a science-derived factor based on the stretch of the universe from when matter first formed until today of 1 million million (1 followed by 12 zeroes, or in scientific notation, 1×10^{12}) to obtain an age for the universe of about 15 BY. His conversion factor converts Creation Time in days to Human Time in days as opposed to our factor, which converts to Human Time in years. Expressed the same way as Dr. Schroeder's conversion factor, the conversion factor derived in Chapter 5 (see Table

5.2) is 0.934 x 10^{12}. This factor is remarkably close to Dr. Schroeder's science-derived factor of 1 x 10^{12}. However, Dr. Schroeder applies the conversion factor without exactly refining the beginning and end times for when God is the conscious observer.

When estimating the time period for each day, Dr. Schroeder points out that his conversion factor is changing as the universe expands, meaning that each day represents a different amount of time in Human Time.

Since the Bible speaks in human terms, Genesis must use an easy-to-understand, constant conversion factor rather than one that varies. Thus, there must be one universal invariant conversion factor, and as such, every creation day is exactly the same period of time, about 2.5 BY.

Given such calculations, and despite a perception that vast and perhaps unresolvable differences remain between science and the Bible, a surprising amount of agreement begins to emerge regarding the age of our universe.

---

[i] (i) Results from NASA's Wilkinson Microwave Anisotropy Probe (WMAP) satellite, launched in 2001, set the age of the universe at 13.75 billion years, plus or minus 130 million years.

(ii) For five-year peer reviewed results see: Gary F. Hinshaw, et al., "Five-Year Wilkinson Microwave Anisotropy Probe Observations: Data Processing, Sky Maps, and Basic Results," *The Astrophysical Journal Supplement* 180/2 (February 2009), pp. 225-245.

(iii) for latest results not yet peer reviewed see: N. Jarosik et al., "Seven-Year Wilkinson Microwave Anisotropy Probe (WMAP) Observations: Sky Maps, Systematic Errors, and Basic Results," *astro-ph* (26 January 2010), arXiv:1001.4744.

(iv) for latest results based on the Hubble space telescope see S. H. Suyu et al., "Dissecting the Gravitational Lens B1608+656. II. Precision Measurements of the Hubble Constant, Spatial

Curvature, and the Dark Energy Equation of State," *The Astrophysical Journal* 711(1) (2010), p. 201.

[2]   Rabbi Aryeh Kaplan, *The Age of the Universe: A Torah True Perspective* (Rueven Meir Caplan, 2008).

[3]   (i) Alexander Poltorak, "On the Age of the Universe", BOr HaTorah Vol. 13, ed. Prof. Herman Branover (Israel: SHAMIR, 1999). Dr. Poltorak performs the calculation assuming two periods of time. His first period is a protophysical period, and the second, once man becomes the conscious observer and collapses the wave function, is a physical period. This author considers the first period to be physical, since it happens during the first six days of creation while God is the conscious observer. When man arrives, he takes over the conscious observer role and determines what happens on earth from then on (according to his clock). God hides and allows man to exercise his free will.

(ii) Alexander Poltorak, "The Age of the Universe Using the Many-Worlds Interpretation," BOr HaTorah Vol. 18, ed. Prof. Herman Bran-over (Israel: SHAMIR, 2008).

[4]   Gerald L. Schroeder, *The Science of God: the Convergence of Scientific and Biblical Wisdom* (New York: Broadway Books, 1997), Chapters 3 and 4.

Chapter 7

Cosmology

Cosmology considers the questions of how the universe began and developed.

These questions date back to age-old creation accounts as well as folklore and mythology. In particular, for the followers of two main world religions, the questions surrounding our origins date back to the creation account found in Genesis. For thousands of years the biblical account was unchallenged. But, as discussed in Chapter 2, more recently it has been questioned and largely rejected by those in the science camp. However, a more detailed study of Genesis offers some intriguing insights that help to answer the questions of our origins.

As noted in previous chapters, the cosmology in Genesis is expounded on and detailed in the Oral Law; it also has been developed in Torah commentaries and Kabbalistic works for hundreds of years to the point that a clear timeline of events can be ascertained.

The first Babylonian astronomers introduced scientific cosmology 4,000 years ago, when they were able to predict the motions of the moon, the planets, and the sun. The Greeks, in the fourth century BCE, were the first to build models to interpret these motions. Today, as is explained in Chapter 3, the Big Bang theory provides a detailed timeline of the events that occurred during the development of the universe.

Do Genesis and science describe the same underlying process of how the universe developed? Do they describe the same developmental events? And do the timing of these events correspond?

The Expanding Universe

The universe has expanded from an infinitesimal size in the beginning of time to its incomprehensible size today. The scientific recognition of an expanding universe is recent. Even though the expanding universe fact can be derived from Einstein's general relativity theory, Einstein himself initially thought the universe was static, neither expanding nor contracting.

In Torah commentaries, the notion of an expanding universe is at least 800 years old. The renowned Torah scholar Ramban clearly described the universe's expansion in his commentary on Genesis. Provided below is that eight-centuries-old description as well as a recent *National Geographic* account of the universe's development. Can you see any significant difference between the two?

At the briefest instant following creation all the matter of the universe was concentrated in a very small place, no larger than a grain of mustard. The matter at this time was very thin, so intangible, that it did not have real substance. It did have, however, a potential to gain substance and form and to become tangible matter. From the initial concentration of this intangible substance in its minute location, the substance expanded, expanding the universe as it did so. As the expansion progressed, a change in the substance occurred. This initially thin non-	Before the big bang, the entire vastness of the observable universe, including all of its matter and radiation, was compressed into a hot, dense mass just a few millimeters across. This nearly incomprehensible state is theorized to have existed for just a fraction of the first second of time...a massive blast allowed all the universe's known matter and energy—even space and time themselves—to spring forth...after the big bang, the universe expanded with incomprehensible speed from its pebble-size origin to astronomical scope. Expansion has apparent-

corporeal substance took on the tangible aspects of matter as we know it. From this initial act of creation, from this ethereally thin pseudosubstance, everything that has existed, or will ever exist, was, is, and will be formed.[1]	ly continued, but much more slowly, over the ensuing billions of years.[2]

Thus, the Torah and science seem to describe a similar process by which the universe develops, that is to say, expands. However, what about key events in the universe's development and their timing? Is there agreement for those as well?

The Events of Days 1 to 4

The Book of Genesis' account of the first four days is both brief and abstract. Nonetheless, with the aid of the biblical sources, it is possible to ascertain and date the key events in the formation of the universe. These can then be compared to predictions of the Big Bang.

Day 1

On Day 1 the first few words of Genesis 1:1 introduces the universe's origins: *"In the beginning of God's creating the heavens and the earth..."*[3] which tells us that at the first moment, God created *from nothing* the basic substance from which he later fashioned the universe.

This first step, as with other creations, is part of a two-step process. First, the basic substance is created, and then the actual physical heaven and earth are formed, as described in Days 1 through 4. The basic substance from which the universe is to be fashioned must consist of the following: (1) what scientists call the elementary particles (objects not known to have substructure) since, by definition, these are the building blocks of everything; and (2) dark matter, since it is also a building block, and moreover we are told, in Isaiah 45:7, that it is a separate creation: *"He who forms the light and creates darkness…"*; and soon after, (3) hydrogen, since we are told, *"With wisdom* [i.e., with hydrogen] *God created…"*[4] (refer to Chapter 5, Godly attributes). Genesis 1:2 also refers to water. In Kabbalah[5] the water element is hydrogen (physical water comprises Kabbalah water [hydrogen] and air [oxygen], i.e., H_2O).

Next, Genesis tells us that there was a period of complete darkness. This darkness is both the absence of light and a separate creation: *"with darkness upon the surface of the deep…"*[6] Following the period of darkness comes a period of pervasive light as *"God said let there be light, and there was light."*[7] As with the period of darkness, this new period of light is expansive: everything is lit up. Then, toward the end of the day, *"God separated between the light and the darkness."*[8] This act of separation must mean there are physical portions of the *sky* that are lit up, and other sections that are dark (as in today's sky). All these steps occur in sequence during Day 1, from 0 to 1.28 BY (see Figure 5.2).

The Big Bang theory describes a similar process to that of Genesis.[9] At first all the key constituents of the universe, up to the very lightest elements (mostly hydrogen), are produced in a very short time. For the following 200 MY (about the first two hours of Creation Time) the Universe exists in the dark ages. During this time all electromagnetic radiation is infrared, and therefore invisible to our eyes, and dark matter and hydrogen are clumped into areas of high density, from which the first stars emerge around 200 MY. These stars are different from our sun: they are short-lived, 100 times bigger, and a million times brighter, and emit much of their radiation in the ultraviolet range. The ultraviolet radiation is so strong that it ionizes the hydrogen in space, and the whole universe appears lit up. The situation changes at about 1 BY, or a couple of hours before the end of Day 1 in Creation Time. Longer-lived and much dimmer stars form in groups, and the gas is no longer ionized, therefore no longer lit up. The universe has developed bright galaxy- or star-filled areas and dark regions.

The above events and those of the subsequent Days 2, 3 and 4 are summarized in Table 7.1 below.

Day 2

Day 2 begins with *"Let there be a firmament... and let it separate between water and water"*[10] and *"God called the firmament 'Heaven.'* *"*[11] Thus, Day 2 is dedicated to separating the waters (i.e., hydrogen) to form the Heavens. Day 2 is the only day where God does not say *"it was good,"* which indicates that what was made on Day 2 was not completed to the point that it was useful to man, or that it had not yet attained its intended state.[12] Many commentary writers have puzzled over the meaning of the Day 2 text. Based on the fact that the subsequent text of Day 3 and 4 identifies the heavens as our night sky and that separating hydrogen into areas of high density is how stars are built, Day 2 is a period of intense star and galaxy formation[13], but these formations do not reach a point of completion that resembles today's useful night sky with all its constellations.

Once again, the creation timeline agrees with the Big Bang theory. Day 2 corresponds to the period between 2.56 BY and 3.84 BY (see Figure 5.3). After the first proto-galaxies appear, the rate of star and galaxy formation begins to increase. The birth rate of stars reaches a peak sometime just before 3 BY and begins to decrease slowly to today's rate of less than 5% of the peak rate.[14] Thus, according to scientists, the main and peak building period of stars and galaxies in the universe occurred during Day 2.

Day 3

Up to this point, the Genesis account has concerned itself with water (hydrogen) and light. Day 3 introduces physical water (therefore oxygen) and earth.[15] The element *earth* corresponds to nitrogen. However, the subsequent text explains that the planet earth and much of life is formed from earth and physical water. Thus earth in Day 3 refers to the physical material from which the land surface is made, and not the element earth (nitrogen). The first part of Day 3 is concerned with gathering the earth and the waters. The latter part of Day 3 focuses on the formation of the physical planet earth.

From a scientific point of view, the text for the first part of Day 3 can be interpreted in a simple and pragmatic manner; it must refer to the gathering of the specific matter from which the earth and the solar system was to be made. However, before all that material can be gathered, the elements must have been formed. Rabbi Yitzchak Ginsburgh explains element formation as described in the Torah[16] as follows:

> Hydrogen corresponds to the sefirah of Wisdom [refer to Chapter 5, Godly Attributes], and that by Wisdom God created all in the universe, as noted in the verse: *"You have made them all with Wisdom"* (Ps. 104:24). This idea—that Wisdom, or its elemental parallel, hydrogen, is the source of all other elements in the universe— corresponds to the accepted contemporary theory of nucleosynthesis[17] (element formation), which theorizes that all elements are created in the fusion reaction of hydrogen in stars. Starting with the first stars, heavy elements formed and drifted through space to find their way to the nebula that formed the Milky Way disk.

Cosmology has shown that at some point our galaxy, the Milky Way, began to form, first its core, and much later its disk. The rich gaseous disk is where our solar system formed. Thus, the text of Day 3 relates that the disk of the Milky Way was formed sometime in the first half of Day 3, between 5.1 and 5.75 BY (see Figure 5.2). This is a tighter estimate than current scientific theory is able to provide. Galaxy formation theory is still being developed, and current estimates hypothesize that the Milky Way disk formed at 5.44±1.8 BY.[18]

The Torah describes and dates key events in the early history of the universe. These events and the times at which they occur are consistent with the Big Bang theory and are summarized in Table 7.1 below.

Table 7.1 Timeline for the Development of the Universe—Torah and Science

Creation event	Creation Time	Human Time	Science event	Science derived time
"In the beginning of God's creating..."		*"the briefest instant following..." time zero*	Early phase of the Big Bang	1st 3 minutes
"With wisdom [i.e., with hydrogen] *God created..."*	Beginning of Day 1		hydrogen appears as the universe expands	3 minutes
"with darkness upon the surface..."			The Dark Age	5–200 MY
"let there be light..."	Day 1 in sequence	0 to 1.28 BY	First stars and the epoch of re-ionization, universe lit up	200–800 MY
"separated between the light and the darkness..."			Infant galaxies, sky with potions of light and darkness	1 BY on

Creation event	Creation Time	Human Time	Science event	Science derived time
"Let there be a firmament…"	Day 2	2.56—3.84 BY	Star birth peak	Peak activity just before 3 BY, then decreases slowly
Gathering the earth and waters, the nebula that formed the Milky Way disk	Day 3 first half	5.11- 5.75 BY	Milky way disk forms	5.44±1.8 BY
Completion of the sun and moon	Day 4, end and into night moon less than 2/3 of hour later	Sun 4.79 BY ago or slightly less	Completion of the Sun	4.57±0.11 BY ago
		Moon less than 70 MY later	Moon	About 50 MY later

Sun, Moon, and Planet Earth

The sun and the moon were created on Day 4. Figure 7.1 shows the timelines for Days 4 and 5, and helps to visualize when the sun and moon formed. This figure includes the three timelines discussed before (Figure 5.2), with the addition of a fourth timeline at the bottom. This fourth timeline is a human timeline running backward from today; it represents Human Time in years ago. Since most events are dated in years past from today (rather than years since the Big Bang), this fourth timeline enables easier referencing for purposes of comparison to science-derived dates. Science-derived events are placed below this timeline for reference.

Events from Science	Human Time (from now running backwards in BY)	Human Time (from start BY)	Divine Time (thousands of years)	Creation Time	Creation Events
	5.01	8.74	27417	DAY 4 — 10	
	4.90	8.84	27708	11	
	4.79	8.95	28000	12	Sun and Moon placed in solar system
Sun 4.57 BY; Moon and Earth younger	3.52	10.23	31500	12	Moon diminished; Earth illuminated
Common ancestor to all current life	3.41	10.33	31792	DAY 5 — 1	Life begins in ocean
	3.30	10.44	32083	2	
	3.20	10.55	32375	3	
	3.09	10.65	32667	4	
	2.98	10.76	32958	5	
	2.88	10.87	33250	6	
	2.77	10.97	33542	7	
	2.66	11.08	33833	8	
	2.56	11.19	34125	9	
	2.45	11.29	34417	10	
	2.34	11.40	34708	11	
First complex organisms	2.24	11.51	35000	12	First filling of the waters in the seas

Figure 7.1 Day 4 (from Hour 10 onward) and Day 5 of Creation

Most of the narrative for Day 4 relates to the utility of the two luminaries: the sun and the moon. Their completion and placement in orbit (i.e., the set-up of the solar system) occurs as the last act of the day, at the end of Day 4.[19] *"And God set them* [the two luminaries] *in the firmament of heaven to give light upon the earth."*[20]

The end of Day 4 in the creation timeline corresponds to 4.79 BY ago (see Figure 7.1). The sources indicate that the sun may have continued to evolve for a short time into the next day:[21] *"Then there was a dispute between the sun and the moon. The moon complained, 'Two kings cannot rule with the same crown.' God became angry and made the moon smaller. The sun was enlarged because it did not enter into the dispute."* Thus, the sun is slightly older (formed less than 4.79 BY ago). The Torah's age for the sun compares well with the best scientific data available, indicating that the sun formed 4.57 ± 0.11 BY ago.[22]

The moon also continues to evolve past the end of Day 4. We learn from Rashi's commentary that the moon is told, "Go and diminish yourself."[23] This happens after the moon is placed. As a result, the moon diminishes and becomes a finished product some time past Day 4. The Pirkê de Rabbi Eliezer[24] specifies that the moon is younger than the sun by no more than 2/3 of an hour, i.e., no more than 70 MY. Scientific theories[25] for the formation of the moon, which continue to be developed, agree with the Torah explanation. They place the moon as younger than the sun by anywhere from 30 to 50 MY. The prevalent theory[26] is that the moon was formed after a giant meteorite impacted the earth and blasted material into orbit around it, and that this material accreted to form the moon. This could indeed be regarded as a diminishing process.

As we saw earlier, according to Genesis the planet earth was formed during Day 3. One of the purposes of the sun is to *"shine upon the earth..."* [27] The Ramban's commentary on Genesis makes it clear that the earth was dark until the sun shone on it:

On the third day, the dry land, seas, and vegetation were created but it was still dark on earth itself. Only on the fourth day were the luminary bodies generated in the realm of the spheres. One of their purposes was to shed light on the earth itself, this light being divided between the sun and the moon, i.e., between day and night.[28]

Thus, we ascertain that God did not observe the planet earth until the light from the sun reached the earth. Therefore, the earth may have been in a non-physical state,[29] because it was unobserved by a conscious observer until it became a physical reality only after the sun was completed and shed light on it. Scientific theory has postulated that the earth was formed about 30 MY later than the sun[30] (i.e. 4.5 to 4.6 BY ago).

Alternatively, a simple interpretation of Genesis indicates that the earth is much older than scientists have determined.

Careful examination of scientific literature on the formation of the sun, the moon and the earth reveals that scientists have accurate and direct measurements for the age of the sun and moon. However, in the case of the earth, scientists have not found a way to determine its age directly, because the earth is a living planet, constantly destroying and recycling old rocks and creating new rock via plate tectonics and volcanism. If there are any of earth's primordial rocks left in their original state, they have not yet been found. Thus, all we can say is that the earth is at least as old as any of its oldest rocks.

The oldest earth rocks date back to about 4 BY ago. Meteorites, which are fragments of asteroids (small celestial bodies composed of rock and metal that move around the sun) that fall to earth, date back to about 4.5 BY ago.[31] Scientists have theorized that the earth formed at the same time as the rest of the solar system, including the asteroids. Thus, scientists take the age of the meteorites found on earth to be the same as the age of the earth.

However, cosmologists have discovered planets that have been ejected from star systems, potentially by a supernova (a very large stellar explosion).[32] Some scientists have postulated that the earth itself was ejected by an earlier solar system.[33] It is also known that nucleosynthesis in stars created enough elements to constitute earth-like planets approximately 8 billion years ago. Thus, the earth could have formed much earlier somewhere in the disk of our galaxy, passed through the clouds of molecular hydrogen and other material from which the solar system was being formed, and been trapped by the gravity of the solar system's material as the system formed 4.5 BY ago. Then, over time asteroids dating back to the formation of the solar system have fallen to earth and in so doing produced the meteorites that we now date. This scenario, which does not contradict the scientific measurement of the age of the earth's rocks (but does contradict the currently accepted theory that the earth formed with the solar system), is consistent with Genesis wherein the planet earth is formed in Day 3[34] (one day earlier than the sun and moon), some 7.5 to 8 BY ago.

Ironically, a controversy that arose owing to literal interpretations of the Bible asserting a young earth, which in no way squared with unfolding scientific evidence for an old earth, has now become a matter of re-examining scientific theory stimulated by a non-literal interpretation of the first six days—and this toward a theory predicting an even older earth!

Finally, the end of Day 4 is also when "*it was good*" appears for the first time in connection with the heavens (i.e., stars). Thus, we ascertain that by about 4.5 BY ago, the night sky looked to the naked eye as it does today, i.e., it had reached the point where it is useful to humankind. Indeed, galaxy observations reveal that by this time galaxies looked like they do today; earlier in time galaxies were smaller and more chaotic in shape.[35]

Thus, the cosmology of Genesis and science seem to be in agreement:

1. An expanding universe that starts from a dense mass just a few millimeters across,

2. A similar sequence of well-defined developmental events that are describable in very similar words (i.e., the first stars lit up the whole universe and there was light), and

3. A close correspondence in the times of all events, except the time of the formation of the earth, which discrepancy can be explained as above.

It is also interesting that, as expected, the main formation events happen during the "daylight" hours of creation days. After an intense first day (first 1.28 BY), there is a quiet "night" where star formation rate starts to increase; this is followed by an intense second day of peak star and galaxy building. During the night after Day 2, star formation continues at a lower rate, and heavy elements continue to form, only to prepare for the building of the Milky Way disk during Day 3. Such a night is once again a quiet period in which the Milky Way develops to the point that the solar system can form in Day 4.

Why should this night be a quiet period in which essentially nothing new happens? In a more corporeal sense, when we are asleep our soul is not in control of our body and we do not create or change anything; however, our bodies continue to function routinely. When God does not exercise His will,[36] it is as if He is asleep, and He does not cause anything new or different to occur. However, what has been created and formed continues to function and develop routinely until the next time God exercises His will.

This pattern of quiet periods, in which God does not exercise His will, is even more apparent in the next two Creation days when life appears.

---

[1] Genesis 1:1, Ramban's interpretation.

[2]   "Origins of the Universe: an Expanding World," *National Geographic*, 1996- 2010 National Geographic Society. http://science.nationalgeographic.com/science/space/universe/origins-universe-article.html.

[3]   Genesis 1:1.

[4]   Psalm 104:24.

[5]   Yitzchak Ginsburgh, *Torah and Chemistry: The Periodic Table of the Elements*, Gal Einai Publication Society.

[6]   Genesis 1:2.

[7]   Genesis 1:3, Malbin's interpretation.

[8]   Genesis 1:4.

[9]   Mark Whittle, *Cosmology: The History and Nature of Our Universe, Course Guidebook* (USA: The Teaching Company, 2008), Themes 3 and 4.

[10]   Genesis 1:6.

[11]   Genesis 1:8.

[12]   Genesis 1:4, Rashi's commentary.

[13]   H. Moose, *In the Beginning: The Bible Unauthorized* (California: Thirty Seven Books, 2001), pp. 90-94.

[14]   Mark Whittle, *Cosmology: The History and Nature of Our Universe, Course Guidebook* (USA: The Teaching Company, 2008), Themes 3 and 4.

[15]   Yitzchak Ginsburgh, *Torah and Chemistry: The Periodic Table of the Elements*, Gal Einai Publication Society.

[16]   Yitzchak Ginsburgh, *Torah and Chemistry: The Periodic Table of the Elements*, Gal Einai Publication Society.

[17]   Nucleosynthesis is the process of creating new atomic nuclei from pre-existing nucleons (protons and neutrons). Nucleosynthesis of the heavier elements required heavy stars and supernova explosions. This theoretically happened as hydrogen and helium from the Big Bang (perhaps influenced by concentrations of dark matter) condensed into the first stars. The elements created in stellar nucleosynthesis range in atomic numbers from six (carbon) to at least 98 (californium), which has been detected in spectra from supernovae. Synthesis of these heavier elements occurs either by nuclear fusion (including both rapid and slow multiple neutron capture) or by nuclear fission, sometimes followed by beta decay.

[18]   Eduardo F. del Peloso, *et al.*, "The Age of the Galactic Thin Disk from Th/Eu Nucleocosmochronology: Extended Sample," *Proceedings of the International Astronomical Union* v.1 (23 December 2005), pp. 485-486 (Cambridge University Press).

[19]   Commentaries place the final steps in the creation and placement of the sun and moon right at the end of Day 4. *"The sun and the moon were hung in a single window during the first three hours of the day."* (Levush, Orach Chayim 428). *"The sun and the moon were created equal, both in size and in brightness, as the Scripture states, 'And God made the two great lights.' They remained equal for twenty-one hours."* (Targum Yonatan; [Rabbi Shmuel Feivel ben Yitzchak Katz] Leket Shmuel, Venice 1694). The original three hours added to these 21 hours totals 24 hours, i.e., the end of Day 4. *"Then there was a dispute between the sun and the moon. The moon complained, 'Two kings cannot rule with the same crown.' God became angry and made the moon smaller. The sun was enlarged because it did not enter into the dispute."* (Chulin 3; Bereishit Rabbah; Zohar Chadash 14c). Both the moon diminishing and the sun enlarging happen at or right after the end of Day 4.

[20]   Genesis 1:17.

[21]   See Endnote 19.

[22]   Alfio Bonanno, Helmut Schlattl and Lucio Paternò, "The Age of the Sun and the Relativistic Corrections in the EOS," *A&A* 390/3 (2002), pp. 1115-1118.

[23]   (i) See Endnote 18.

    (ii) Rashi's commentary on the verse "*And God said: Let there be luminaries in the heavens*" (Genesis 1:14). The Talmud (bHul 60b) quotes Rabbi Shimon ben Pazi: "It is first written 'the two great luminaries,' and then it is written 'the great luminary and the small luminary.' How is this explained? The Moon said to the Almighty: 'Master of the World, is it possible for two kings to rule under one crown?' The Almighty replied: 'Go and diminish yourself.' "

[24]   Michael Friedlander, *Pirkê de Rabbi Eliezer* [part of the oral law], (Illinois: Varda Books, 2004), Chapter 7 says that the sun is older than the moon by a period of less than 2/3 of an hour, or 70 MY.

[25]   Thorsten Klein *et al.*, "Hf–W Chronometry of Lunar Metals and the Age and Early Differentiation of the Moon," *Science Magazine* 310/5754, 2005, pp. 1671–1674.

[26]   Edward Belbruno and J. Richard Gott III, "Where Did The Moon Come From?" *The Astronomical Journal* 129 (3) (2005), pp. 1724–1745.

[27]   Genesis 1:15.

[28]   Ramban's commentary on Genesis 1:15.

[29]   Alexander Poltorak, "On the Age of the Universe," BOr HaTorah Vol. 13, ed. Prof. Herman Branover (Israel: SHAMIR, 1999).

[30]   Brent Dalrymple, *The Age of the Earth* (California: Stanford University Press, 1991).

[31]   Ibid.

[32]   Marcos C. de La Fuente and Marcos R. de La Fuente, "Runaway Planets," *New Astronomy* v. 4, no. 1 (February 1999), pp. 21-32.

[33]   Rhawn, Joseph, and Rudolf Schild, "Biological Cosmology and the Origins of Life in the Universe," *Journal of Cosmology* v. 5 (January 30, 2010), pp. 1040-1090.

[34]   H. Moose, *In the Beginning: The Bible Unauthorized* (California: Thirty Seven Books, 2001), pp. 94-95.

[35]   L.S. Sparke and J.S. Gallagher III, *Galaxies in the Universe: An Introduction,* Second Edition (Cambridge, UK: Cambridge University Press, 2007), pp. 397-402

[36]   Rabbi Menachem M. Schneerson, *Likkutei Sichot—Volume VII: Shmos* (New York: Kehot Publication Society, 1996).

Chapter 8

The Appearance of Life on Earth

What is life?

Encyclopaedia Britannica offers this definition:

> Matter characterized by the ability to metabolize nutrients (process materials for energy and tissue building), grow, reproduce, and respond and adapt to environmental stimuli.

Again, the creation account in Genesis speaking to the origin of life and its appearance on earth is fundamental to both Judaism and Christianity. The Genesis account is expounded and detailed in the Oral Law and has been further developed in commentaries and Kabbalistic works over thousands of years.

The Bible provides significantly more material on life, and in particular on humankind, than on cosmology. Thus, it is possible to develop a clear timeline for the appearance of and the extinction (as will be discussed in the next chapter) of life on earth. Genesis deals with four major classifications of life: microscopic, plant, animal, and humankind. It does not, unfortunately, provide any significant breakdown between various plants or animal species.

Over time, humans began to study life in a logical manner that came to be called biology, a natural science concerned with the study of life and living organisms. The origins of modern biology and its approach to the study of nature are most often traced back to ancient Greece. The classification of living things into animals and plants is ancient. Aristotle (384 BCE–322 BCE) classified animal species in his work *The History of Animals*, and his pupil Theophrastus (c. 371–c. 287 BCE) wrote a parallel work on plants (*The History of Plants*).

In 1674, Antonie van Leeuwenhoek, often called the father of microscopy, sent to the Royal Society of London a copy of his first observations of microscopic single-celled organisms. Up to this time, the existence of such miniscule organisms was unknown. His discoveries opened the human mind to consider more broadly the implications of life and its origins.

Today biology has developed a good understanding of the diverse array of living organisms that are found on earth, which includes plants, animals, fungi, bacteria, *et al.* The properties common to these organisms are a carbon- and water-based cellular form with complex organization and heritable genetic information. Biology relies on classification within a hierarchical structure, or taxonomy. Each level in this hierarchical order is called rank. At the top of the hierarchy is life, followed by several levels of further subdivision. At the second highest rank, the kingdom level of classification, there are at least six subdivisions. These include the familiar plants, animals, and bacteria, and three more subdivisions (e.g., fungi, which include mushrooms). Humankind is classified as belonging to the animal kingdom. At the lowest level are species, defined as a group of organisms capable of interbreeding and producing fertile offspring. There are millions of species.

The fossil record clearly documents the appearance of life on earth, and evolution is the scientific theory to explain how life developed.

Do Genesis and science describe the same underlying process of life's development? Do they describe the same sequence for the appearance of life on earth? And what about the times at which different life forms appeared—do they match?

There is clear disagreement in the descriptions of how life develops provided by science and Genesis. In science, the theory of evolution specifies a purely materialistic process driven by the natural selection of random variation at the genetic level. A key process in evolution is speciation, in which a single ancestral species splits and diversifies into multiple new species. Ultimately, all living (and extinct) species are descended from a common ancestor via a long series of evolutionary events.

In Genesis, microscopic life is first formed, and macroscopic life is then created and formed, "*each according to its kind.*"[1] We will study later in this chapter what *kind* might mean; however, it is clear that there is no speciation in the scientific meaning; instead each living kind is made separately. Humankind in particular is a different creation. Having said that each kind is made separately, they are all made by one Creator, and as such they can appear to have evolved from each other. If we walk down the street and study cars, we discover a clear evolutionary sequence; we can date each car and see how improvements were made as models appeared. The basic model became a sports car to go fast, or a large car to carry more loads, and so on. What appears as an evolutionary sequence is actually made by one or more designers.

Despite this disagreement in the descriptions of how life develops provided by science and Genesis, with the aid of the fossil record, we are able to set the difference aside and focus on the timeline for the appearance of life on earth (e.g., examine each model and when it appeared). Because the fossil record provides a process (e.g., theory of evolution) independent timeline of the appearance on life on earth, and Genesis also provides a timeline for the appearance of life on earth, we are able to conduct a timeline comparison.

We will begin with land-based plant life and then investigate the other forms of life (except for humankind, which is dealt with in Chapter 10).

The discussion in this chapter is illustrated with Figure 7.1—showing the timelines for Day 4 and Day 5 of Creation, and Figure 8.1 below—showing a timeline for Day 6 of Creation. As explained previously, the fourth timeline in the figures is identical to the human timeline (the third timeline), with the adaptation that it reports times in reverse, starting at 0 as the current time, and running to the beginning of creation at 13.74 BY ago. Note this fourth timeline in Figure 8.1 shows time as zero at Hour 10 of Day 6 vs. at today. The reason for this is that the time between today and Hour 10 is 5,773 years, while the time between Hour 10 and earlier events is millions of years, and thus the 5,773 years are inconsequential.

As we saw in Chapter 5 (the creation timeline section), the Talmud provides precise information, hour by hour, for Day 6, with respect to man's formation/creation and his and her subsequent human activities. This information, depicted at the top of Figure 8.1, is useful in pinpointing the full timeline for the appearance of macroscopic life on earth.

Creation Events	Creation Time	Divine Time (thousands of years)	Human Time (from start BY)	Human Time (from now running backwards in BY)	Events from Science
	12	38500	12.78	0.96	
Dust was gathered	1	38792	12.89	0.85	
Dust kneaded into shapeless mess; Formation of complex life begins	2	39083	13.00	0.75	
Adam's limbs shaped	3	39375	13.10	0.64	
Soul infused into Adam	4	39667	13.21	0.53	Cambrian Explosion
Adam rose and stood on his feet	5	39958	13.32	0.43	First fish
Adam named the animals	6	40250	13.42	0.32	Primitive plants. Four-legged animals
Eve was created	7	40542	13.53	0.21	Seeds, plants and trees diversify
Cain and Abel born. Garden is planted after man created.	8	40833	13.64	0.11	Flowering plants Modern birds
Adam and Eve are commanded to not eat from the Tree	9	41125	13.74	0.0	Age of universe 13.7
Adam and Eve sinned	10	41417			
Adam and Eve were tried	11	41708			
Adam and Eve were expelled from the Garden	12	42000			

DAY 6 (hours)

Figure 8.1 Day 6 of Creation

Land Plants

Plants, like all creations and formations, are brought into existence via two operations (see Chapter 5 key concepts—a two-step process). The earth is first invested with the power to grow, or give life to, the seeds sown on it. The second operation is to form the actual physical vegetation. The earth is then able to grow this vegetation on its surface. In Day 3 the text says, "*Let the earth sprout vegetation*,"[2] i.e., "*Let it endow itself with the power to grow grass…*"[3] In Day 6 the text says, "*And all the herb of the field had not yet sprouted, for God had not sent rain upon the earth and there was no man to work the soil.*"[4] It is clear there is no vegetation sprouting above the surface of the earth until Day 6; only then, after man is completed, does it physically sprout and start to leave evidence in the fossil record.[5]

The text continues, telling us that that vegetation, and in particular trees, start appearing:

> *God planted a garden toward the east, in Eden; and there He placed the man whom He had formed. And God caused to sprout from the ground every tree that was pleasing to the sight and good for food; the Tree of life also in the midst of the garden, and the Tree of the Knowledge of Good and Bad.*[6]

Finally, we are clearly told that plants and trees have appeared by the time Adam is commanded not to eat of the Tree of the Knowledge of Good and Evil: "*God took man and placed him in the Garden of Eden, to work it and guard it* [i.e., the garden was complete]. *And God commanded the man…*"[7]

Thus, according to Genesis, plants begin to appear above the surface of the earth directly after man is completed at the beginning of Hour 6 (that is, four hours before the sin), and have appeared by the time Adam and Eve are commanded not to eat from the tree, or Hour 9 (one hour before the sin); see Figure 8.1. An hour is approximately 106.5 million years (MY); see table 5.2, which indicates that plants appear between 426 and 106 million years ago (Ma). The Torah times for the appearance of plant life match very well with scientific evidence from the fossil record,[8] as shown in Table 8.1. The two right-hand columns in Table 8.1 are extracted from the timeline for appearance of life on earth as summarized in Table 3.2.

Table 8.1 Timeline for the Appearance of Land Plants— The Torah and Science

Creation event	Creation Time	Human Time	Science event	Science derived time
Man completed; God has begun planting the garden	beginning of Hour 6	soon after 426 Ma	first primitive macroscopic plants appear on land	420 Ma
"God caused to sprout from the ground every tree..."			seed plants and conifers diversify	280 Ma
Garden completed, *"God commanded..."*	by end of Hour 9	by 106.5 Ma	flowering plants appear	130 Ma

The Beginnings of Life

The Torah clearly places the first life in the waters on Day 5. This creation proceeds in three steps (see Chapter 5 key concepts —a two-step process). Exactly at the beginning of the day, *"let the waters teem with teaming living creatures, and fowl that fly about over the earth..."*[9] meaning *"let the waters bring forth animating power: the power to instill life in those creatures whose medium was to be the water."*[10] This is immediately followed by *"and God created the great sea giants and every living being that creeps, with which the waters teemed after their kinds..."*[11]

Finally, exactly at the end of Day 5, *"Be fruitful and multiply, and fill the waters in the seas; but the fowl shall increase on earth."*[12] Therefore, the essence of life appears at the beginning of Day 5 (3.52 BY ago), and marine life seems to multiply and therefore appear at the end of Day 5 (2.24 BY ago); see Figure 7.1.

The appearance of the essence of life in the Torah corresponds almost exactly with the scientifically derived date for the appearance of life on earth. The last universal ancestor,[13] the name given to the hypothetical single cellular organism or single cell from which all organisms now living on earth descend, is estimated to have lived some 3.5 to 3.8 BY ago.

The appearance of marine life is a more difficult topic. The phrase *"and it was so"* appears repeatedly in the creation account. Commentaries have explained that this phrase signifies that the creation/formation appearing before the phrase became eternally established.[14]

Day 5 is the only day of creation in which the phrase *"and it was so"* does not appear. Commentaries[15] have argued that this means that (i) the physical bodies of creatures that were created did not continue to exist in the form originally created, and (ii) that the living beings created on Day 5 were completed the next day. As such they could not multiply until their completion on Day 6. Thus, marine life of any significant size and mobility must appear on Day 6. This interpretation is reinforced further by the specific Hebrew word used in the next formation of life, the formation of animals in Day 6. The Day 6 text on the formation of animals includes the root "asah." This root indicates the completion of something that already exists,[16] an allusion to the animals of the seas being completed in Day 6. However, the time (2.24 BY ago) of the Day 5 blessing *"fill the waters in the seas"* does match with one of the most significant events in the development of life on earth according to scientists: 2.2 BY ago, oxygen in the atmosphere increased dramatically, and the first complex microorganisms appeared,[17] with cells containing complex structures inside their membranes.

Complex Life

The formation of life in Day 6 proceeds in a two-step process. First, "*Let the earth bring forth living creatures, each according to its kind: animal*[18] *and creeping being, and the beasts of the land each according to its kind*"[19] meaning, "*Let the earth bring forth life to animate all animals.*"[20] The microscopic multi-cellular life from which the second operation can proceed is made first. Second, "*God made the beast of the earth according to its kind, and the animal according to its kind and every creeping being of the ground according to its kind.*"[21] This second operation, the essential formation of animals, occurs before the next creation (i.e., the completion of man infused with his Godly soul) in hours 1 to 4 on Day 6. At the end of Hour 4, the fundamental formation of animals must be complete, and in particular, as discussed above, the sea animals must be completed.

However, the formation of life does not end at the conclusion of Hour 4; it continues, perhaps right up to the end of Day 6, when creation ends. When the potential for life is brought forth, the potential for four formations is brought forth: living creatures, animal, beast, and creeping beings.[22] However, when the first physical formation occurs (at the end of Hour 4), only three items are formed: beast, animal, and creeping being.[23] The commentaries[24] have difficulty decisively explaining this transition from four items to three items. When Adam is blessed, well after he is created and before he sins,[25] God says, "*Be fruitful and multiply, fill the earth and subdue it; and rule over the fish of the sea, the bird of the sky and every living thing that moves on the earth.*"[26] The description "*every living thing that moves on the earth*" is much more encompassing than the three items used to describe the physical formation of life earlier in Genesis.[27] The sages teach that each word change in the Torah provides new information. Thus, at the beginning of the day the potential for all life from earth is first brought forth,[28] and then by the end of Hour 4 some, but not all, life is formed.[29] The remainder of life is formed after the end of Hour 4, potentially right up to the point when creation stops (i.e., 5,773 years ago).

Further evidence indicating that not all life is formed by the end of Hour 4 is found by comparing the Day 6 description of life with the description of the same life when it is brought on board Noah's ark. Day 6: *"God made the beast of the earth according to its kind, and the animal according to its kind and every creeping being of the ground according to its kind."*[30] Noah—*"they and every beast after its kind, every animal after its kind, every creeping thing that creeps on the earth after its kind..."*[31] Between the two accounts the main change is the replacement of word *the* with the word *every* in front of beast and animal, clearly indicating that there are more species formed after Hour 4 of Day 6.

Finally, the fact that Adam, and not God, named the animals provides a key clue as to the time of their formation. The creation text repeatedly says *"God called"* the light day, the firmament heaven, the dry land earth, etc. Yet when it comes to three particular formations, *"the beasts of the field," "the cattle"* and *"the birds of the sky,"*[32] God commands Adam to name them. Some commentaries[33] interpret this to mean that what Adam named was made after Adam was completed, while what was made before Adam was called (i.e., named) by God. Thus the three items above were made during Hour 6, after Adam is completed at end of Hour 5 and just in time for Adam to name them.

A similar situation occurs with fish. There is no specific mention of fish on Day 5. Even if their creation is included in Day 5, they are formed or completed only on Day 6 and only after the end of Hour 4. After completion they multiply per their blessing on Day 5.[34] The Torah does not mention fish directly until Adam is blessed on Day 6. God says to Adam, *"Be fruitful and multiply, fill the earth and subdue it; and rule over the fish of the sea..."*[35] Thus, fish appear after the end of Hour 4.

Birds follow the same pattern. Birds or fowl are first introduced in Day 5. However, the text *"but the fowl shall increase on earth*[36] clearly explains that they will not reproduce until Day 6. Furthermore, on Day 6, prior to Adam's naming certain species, the text says *"Now, God had formed out of the ground every beast of the field and every bird of the sky…"*[37] indicating that the birds were made from the earth, a clear reference to formation on Day 6. The Genesis text does not indicate exactly when the birds multiplied on Day 6 (per their blessing given on Day 5[38]), but it must be sometime in the last several hours of Day 6.

The Torah also provides an important clue as to the first formation of animals. Rashi[39] explains that the inhabitants of the earth were created with the Godly attribute of mercy. This attribute of mercy first appears in Genesis 2.4. As discussed earlier, in biology, taxonomy is the practice and science of classification, and rank is the level (the relative position) in a taxonomic hierarchy. There are several levels of classification between life and species. The phylum level corresponds to a group of organisms with a certain degree of morphological or developmental similarity. Morphology includes aspects of the outward appearance (shape, structure, color, and pattern) as well as the form and structure of the internal parts, like bones and organs. There are well under one hundred phyla accounting for over one million animal species.

The biological taxonomic hierarchy, like everything else in nature, corresponds to the ten sefirot, and in particular (as discussed in Chapter 5), the biological classification level of phylum corresponds to the Godly attribute of mercy.[40] Thus, it is expected that the first formation of life—which is done with the first emotive sefirah, mercy—should produce the phylum for all future species. At the end of Hour 4 we expect all phyla to appear.

Using Figure 8.1, one can place the above-mentioned events on the Human Time timeline. Table 8.2 summarizes the Torah-derived times for the appearance of complex life (Human Time column) and compares it to the science-derived times (science event column).[41]

Table 8.2 Times for the Appearance of Life—Torah and Science

Creation event	Creation Time	Human Time	Science event	Notes
first life in the waters	Day 5 beginning	3.52 BY ago	last universal ancestor appears approximately 3.5 BY ago	in Torah this is also the essence of life
waters filled with life	Day 5 end	2.24 BY ago	cells containing complex structures appear approximately 2.2 BY ago	oxygen in the atmosphere increases dramatically at this time
beginning of complex life	Day 6 Hour 1	959--- Ma	multi-cellular life appears starting 900 Ma	
			first animal fossils 610 Ma	

Creation event	Creation Time	Human Time	Science event	Notes
essential formation of animals and completion of sea animals	end of Hour 4	532 Ma	Cambrian explosion where all but one modern phylum of animal life made a first appearance in the fossil record about 530 Ma and within a relatively short period of time	Invertebrates appear during the Cambrian explosion, many of which are well described by "*creeping being*"
other animals, fish, and birds completed after this time				
formation and naming of the cattle, the birds, and every beast of the field	Hour 6	426-320 Ma	first four-legged animals appeared 397 Ma	
			first four-legged herbivores appeared by 360 Ma	commentaries (Ramban) indicate that herbivores correspond to cattle and carnivores to beasts
			fossil forefathers of modern mammals, birds, and reptiles appeared by 310 Ma	birds formed by the time Adam names them, may not have multiplied yet

Creation event	Creation Time	Human Time	Science event	Notes
latest time for completion of the fish, the bird, and every living thing that moves on earth	prior to the end of the creation process	5,773 years ago	first fish starting 450 Ma	fish began to be formed after the end of Hour 4, i.e., after 500 Ma
			first mammals 215 Ma	
			modern birds 150 Ma, etc.	birds multiplied after they were named?

The Torah and science agree on the timeline for the appearance of life. After the appearance of first life and complex organisms, the next and most important milestone of the appearance of life is the Cambrian explosion,[42] during which all but one modern phylum of animal life first appeared in the fossil record. The Cambrian explosion corresponds exactly with the Torah's main formation of life prior to the creation of man, i.e., the end of Hour 4. The subsequent history of animal life amounts to little more than variations on anatomical themes established during the Cambrian explosion, within five to at most fifty million years, i.e., three to at most thirty minutes of Creation Time.

After the Cambrian period, the next milestone is when Adam *"assigned names to all the cattle and to the birds of the sky and to every beast of the field..."*[43] The time of the naming (which as discussed above is also the time these animals are formed) coincides with the appearance of four-legged herbivores (cattle, according to Ramban) and carnivores (beasts, according to Ramban). By the time Adam completes his naming task, all animals that are fossil forefathers of modern mammals, birds, and reptiles have appeared. Following the naming, the Torah does not provide any more exact times for the appearance of life (until the end of Day 6, by which time all species have appeared). However, the appearance of life forms, such as fish and birds, is chronologically consistent with the Torah text.

The Genesis account of the appearance of life on earth repeatedly uses the term *"according to its kind."* The commentaries have interpreted the term *kind* to mean species. Species is a particular unit of biological classification at a very detailed level (there are millions of identified species). The analysis above suggests that species were formed throughout Day 6. Thus, the actual creatures that Adam named hundreds of millions of years ago were not the same as those we observe today; more and more species continued to be formed after the naming.

Finally, further development has and continues to occur in the case of other creations or formations. Nothing is created or formed statically. The planet earth continues to change due to plate tectonics, volcanism, climate change, etc., and the universe continues to evolve and form new stars. Therefore, it is not inconsistent for the animal kingdom to also continue to develop/adapt as it does, although according to Genesis, kinds cannot become other kinds.

In conclusion, despite different descriptions provided by scientists and the Genesis narrative regarding how life develops, each provides a timeline for the appearance of life, and the two are in agreement on these matters:

1. First appearance of microscopic life in waters,

2. Main life-appearance event at a specific time, whereby life forms appear over a very short time (Cambrian explosion),

3. More gradual appearance of many species following this main life-appearance event, and

4. Virtually exact time correspondence for the first two events (items 1 and 2) with no inconsistency as to the time of appearance for the rest of life (for Humankind see Chapter 10).

Finally, as we saw in Chapter 7—Cosmology, there is a curious spacing to events. As discussed in Chapter 3, those who study science have marveled at the discrete set of events that leads to life, with large billion-year periods between which virtually nothing happens. The creation account is consistent with these long periods between short and profound life formation events. There are three key life appearance events: 3.5 BY ago (corresponding to the beginning of Day 5), 2.2 BY ago (corresponding to the end of Day 5), and 532 Ma (corresponding to the end of Hour 4, Day 6), followed by a continuous sequence of further appearances of life (corresponding to the rest of the daylight hours of day 6). These life-formation events correspond precisely with the times when God exercises His will; between these times, nothing significantly novel worthy of mention in a very short creation narrative is happening.

So far we have dealt with the appearance of life on earth. As we shall see in the next chapter, this is only half the story.

---

[1]   Genesis 1:24.

[2]   Genesis 1:11.

[3]   H. Moose, *In the Beginning: The Bible Unauthorized* (California: Thirty Seven Books, 2001), pp. 96-97. Other sources (Talmud Chullim 60b, Midrash Rabbah 12:4, Rashi on Genesis 2:5) do say there was vegetation on Day 3, but it remained below the earth's surface until Day 6, when it sprouted above the earth's surface and began to grow, produce seed, and die, and therefore began to show up in the fossil record.

[4]   Genesis 2:5. Malbim (Mendel Weinbach, Reuven Subar, *The Essential Malbim* (New York: Mesorah Publications Ltd., 2009), p. 24) explains that the "rain" described in this verse is divine rain, matar in Hebrew, which descends in response to man's prayers. This divine rain is different from natural rain which descends as a result of water vapour ascending to form clouds. Scientifically it is known that natural rain had occurred on earth well before the appearance of vegetation. However, vegetation did not grow until the divine rain descended.

[5]   H. Moose, *In the Beginning: The Bible Unauthorized* (California: Thirty Seven Books, 2001), p. 159.

[6]   Genesis 2:8 and 2:9.

[7]   Genesis 2:15 and 2:16.

[8]   (i) Michael Marshall, "Timeline: The Evolution of Life," *New Scientist*, 14 July 2009.

        (ii) For more details see Stephen Jay Gould, *The Book of Life: An Illustrated History of the Evolution of Life on Earth*, Second Edition (New York: W. W. Norton Inc., 2001).

[9]   Genesis 1:20.

[10]   H. Moose, *In the Beginning: The Bible Unauthorized* (California: Thirty Seven Books, 2001), p. 105.

[11]   Genesis 1:21; Rashi says creeping being means "something that does not rise much above the ground and has a method of locomotion that is not discernable."

[12]   Genesis 1:22.

[13]   (i) W. Ford Doolittle, "Uprooting the Tree of Life," *Scientific American* 282(2), February 2000, pp. 90-95.

(ii) Theobald, Douglas L, "A Formal Test of the Theory of Universal Common Ancestry," *Nature* 465 (7295) (13 May 2010), pp. 219–222.

[14]   Rashbam on Genesis 1.

[15]   Rabbi Meir Zlotowitz, Bereishis, *Genesis / A New Translation with a Commentary Anthologized from Talmudic Midrashic and Rabbinic Sources* (New York: Mesorah Publications Ltd., 1977)

(i) Ramban on Genesis 1:20, the absence of "and it was so" means "did not continue to exist in the form originally created."

(ii) Malbun on Genesis 1:20, "in addition it does not say and it was so because the creation of living beings was not completed until the 6th day the works of the 5th day were a prelude to that which was completed on the 6th day."

[16]   Mendel Weinbach, Reuven Subar, *The Essential Malbim* (New York: Mesorah Publications Ltd., 2009), p. 25.

[17]   (i) For information on the rapid appearance of oxygen on earth see James F. Kasting and Shuhei Ono, "Palaeoclimates: The First Two Billion Years," *Philosophical Transactions of the Royal Society B*, v.361/1470, (2006), pp. 917-929.

(ii) For information of the appearance of complex multi-cellular life see Blair S. Hedges *et al.*, "A Molecular Timescale of Eukaryote Evolution and the Rise of Complex Multicellular Life," *BMC Evolutionary Biology* v.4 Issue 1 (2004).

[18]   The word for *animal* in the Torah may not have the same meaning as defined by science thousands of years later.

[19]   Genesis 1:24.

[20]   H. Moose, *In the Beginning: The Bible Unauthorized* (California: Thirty Seven Books, 2001), p. 109.

[21]   Genesis 1:25.

22   Genesis 1:24.

23   Genesis 1:25.

24   Wilfred Shuchat, *The Creation According to the Midrash Rabbah* (Israel: Devora Publishing, 2002), p. 266.

25   (i) After Adam is created we learn that he is to be *"fruitful and multiply, fill the earth..."* [Genesis 1:28]. The exact timing of this blessing is not provided by the Talmud reference on Day 6 [Babylonian Talmud, Sanhedrin 38b].

(ii) Michael Friedlander, *Pirkê de Rabbi Eliezer* (Illinois: Varda Books, 2004), Chapter 12, says "The Holy One, blessed be He, made ten wedding canopies for Adam in the garden of Eden..." "What is the custom observed by the precentor? He stands and blesses the bride in the midst of her wedding chamber. Likewise the Holy One, blessed be He, stood and blessed Adam and his help-mate, as it is said, 'And God blessed them...' " (Genesis 1:28). This elaboration of events from the oral tradition makes it clear that Adam and Eve were blessed in the garden and therefore before the sin. After the sin, Genesis is clear that the only actions are that Adam and Eve are judged and then expelled from the garden.

26   Genesis 1:28.

27   Genesis 1:25.

28   Genesis 1:24.

29   Genesis 1:25.

30   Genesis 1:25.

31   Genesis 7:14.

32   Genesis 2:19–20.

33   Ramban on Genesis 1:3 discussing commentary by Ibn Ezra.

34 Genesis 1:22.

35 Genesis 1:28.

36 Genesis 1:22.

37 Genesis 2:19.

38 Genesis 1:22.

39 Rashi on Genesis 2:4. See Rabbi Meir Zlotowitz, Bereishis, *Genesis / A New Translation with a Commentary Anthologized from Talmudic Midrashic and Rabbinic Sources* (New York: Mesorah Publications Ltd., 1977), p. 87.

40 Yitzchak Ginsburgh, *Life Sciences: Torah and Taxonomy*, Gal Einai Publication Society.

41 (i) Michael Marshall, "Timeline: The Evolution of Life," *New Scientist*, 14 July 2009.

(ii) For more details see: Stephen Jay Gould, *The Book of Life: An Illustrated History of the Evolution of Life on Earth*, Second Edition (New York: W. W. Norton Inc., 2001).

42 Stephen Jay Gould, "The Evolution of Life on Earth," *Scientific American*, October 1994, pp. 85-91.

43 Genesis 2:20.

Chapter 9

Mass Extinctions of Life on Earth

As much as by the appearance of new species, the history of
life on earth is punctuated by extinctions, and in particular, by several mass extinctions.

Extinction is the end of an organism or group of organisms,
typically a species. The moment of extinction is generally considered to come with the death of the last individual instance of the
group. Because the geographical area within which species can be
found may be very large, determining this moment is difficult; it is
usually determined retrospectively. Such determinations notwith-
standing, extinctions are very common: the vast majority of species
ever to have lived are now extinct.

Species regularly become extinct. When extinction is considered over time and prior to the effects of humankind, an average
rate of extinction, referred to as the background extinction rate
(e.g., at the background rate one species of bird goes extinct every
estimated 400 years), is discernible. However, from the time since
life began on earth, several unusually large extinctions have occurred, each involving the demise of vast numbers of species.
These events are called extinction events or mass extinctions. Each
extinction event occurred over a relatively short period of time,
during which the number of species that went extinct was significantly higher than that to be expected for that period of time based
on the background extinction rate. The most recent extinction
event, best known for the demise of the dinosaurs, was a large-
scale mass extinction of animal and plant species in a geologically
short period of time approximately 65.5 million years ago (Ma). In
the past 540 million years it is generally agreed[1] that there have

been five extinction events when over 50% of animal species at the time died.

How do we know mass extinctions have occurred?

As we saw in Chapter 3, the fossil record provides us with a remarkable chronicle of life on earth. However, even large-scale extinctions seldom generate large deposits of bones[2] where paleontologists might expect to find the last instances of a species. No paleontologist would ever claim that a particular fossil specimen represents the very last survivor of a species—the probability of this last individual occurrence being fossilized, discovered, and collected is infinitesimally small. Nevertheless, repeated investigation of the fossil record does allow scientists to corroborate and refine assessments of when a species became extinct. We can, for instance, be confident that a particular species became extinct at or before a certain time when intensive sampling of younger rocks fails to produce members of that species. Thus, the fossil record reveals a detailed timeline for extinctions, and in particular, the five major extinctions of life on earth.

So far we have simply described what is observed in the fossil record. Scientists view extinctions as naturally occurring events (i.e., the effect of some cause, like a meteor impact). Recently, humankind has been responsible for certain extinctions (e.g., by over-hunting and deforestation), and some argue a major extinction is occurring now as modern life profoundly affects our planet through pollution and waste; nonetheless, historically documented mass extinctions preceded humankind (but as we shall see, not Adam).

How do these natural events occur? There is ongoing debate about the causes of all mass extinctions. The so-called press / pulse model[3] postulates that mass extinctions generally require two types of cause: long-term pressure on the ecosystem (press) and a sudden catastrophe (pulse) toward the end of the pressure period. Press disturbances place multigenerational stress on ecosystems; pulse disturbances are sudden, catastrophic, and cause extensive mortality. An example of a press disturbance is climate change, while a meteor impact is an example of a pulse disturbance.

What does the Torah say about extinctions? At first glance, nothing at all. As we saw in Chapter 8, Genesis seems simply to discuss the appearance of life on earth. However, a closer examination of Genesis, the Oral Law, and the commentaries reveals a rich timeline for the major extinctions of life on earth. Furthermore, it reveals that Adam, and later Eve, were major players in the five mass extinctions.

This chapter develops the biblical cause and time of each of the five major extinctions of life and compares biblical times to the science-derived times for the extinctions. We begin with the most recent extinction, which turns out to be a direct result of Adam's sin.

Impact of the Sin on Plant and Animal Life—The Last Major Extinction

After Adam is commanded not to eat from the Tree of the Knowledge of Good and Bad, the events leading up the sin (i.e., to Adam eating the fruit from the tree) unfold over a period of one creation hour (see Figure 8.1), corresponding to the last 106 million years.

There are four key characters that play a role in Adam's sin: the serpent, Eve, the earth, and Adam. At the moment of sin everything changes, for humans in particular. The process leading to sin is begun by the serpent, who convinces Eve to partake of the fruit. Eve, in turn, insists that Adam eat some fruit. Later in the narrative, when Adam and Eve are judged by God, it is made clear that the earth also had a role in the sin. The Oral Law tells us that "*Because it* [the earth] *did not speak out* [by protesting and warning Adam] *against the evil deed* [the sin] *it was cursed.*"[4]

We first describe the nature of the serpent, as well as review the consequences of Adam's sin. Then we explain the effect of the

consequences on plant and animal life. These effects and their timing, as derived from the Torah, are compared to scientific
knowledge of the same events and their science-derived times.

The Serpent

The serpent is a snake with legs that does not speak with a
human voice. The serpent is referred to by the Hebrew word *na-
chash*,[5] which is the same Hebrew word generally used in the Torah
narrative to describe regular snakes. As such, there is no special
name for the serpent in the story of Adam and Eve as compared
to other snakes mentioned in the Torah. Further, the serpent's
punishment for its part in the sin included this passage: *"upon your
belly shall you go..."*[6] which indicates that it originally had legs that
were subsequently removed. The commentaries explain that prior
to Adam's sin, Adam and Eve could understand what the animals
were saying, and the serpent communicated with Eve in its own
language and/or by its actions.[7] Further evidence that the snake
does not speak with a human voice can be found by comparing
the Genesis text *"The serpent said to the woman..."*[8] to the only other
biblical text describing an animal that speaks. In Numbers the text
"God opened the mouth of the she-donkey and it said to Balaam..."[9] describes a speaking donkey which, in a most unusual miracle, is
granted the power of speech.[10] The Balaam story occurs long after
the sin when humans cannot understand animals, unless they
speak with a human voice.

Although there are many more complex descriptions of the
serpent, a consensus of commentaries agrees with the interpretation provided above.[11] The serpent was at first a regular snake with
legs.

Consequences and Judgments

Following Adam's sin, God descended into the Garden of Eden, judged Adam and Eve, and pronounced the consequences of their role in the sin to the serpent and the earth.

In the case of Adam and Eve, God carried out a dialogue with each of them separately to discover what had happened, and based on their explanation, he pronounced his judgment[12] (after the sin). This logical consequence process follows the due process of breaking a law, being interrogated as to circumstances and reasons for the actions, and then being judged accordingly. The serpent and the earth are not judged. God did not have dialogue with them; He simply stated the natural consequences that resulted from their actions. Unlike logical consequences, natural consequences occur immediately (e.g., one goes outside without a coat and feels cold). In the case of the serpent—it loses its legs and must crawl on its belly. As for the case of the earth—it is cursed.[13] These natural consequences took effect at the point when the action or inaction occurred,[14] before the actual sin.

The natural consequence to the earth is the curse, which begins immediately upon the earth's non-action. The curse is complex; however, key details can be ascertained from God's words to Adam.[15]

> *To Adam He said... accursed is the ground because of you; through suffering shall you eat of it all the days of your life. Thorns and thistles shall it sprout for you, and you shall eat the herb of the field. By the sweat of your brow shall you eat bread...*

The commentaries interpret the meaning of these words for us: *"accursed is the ground because of you"*—meaning for your sake the earth will yield harvest, but only in scant measure—many seeds sown will never sprout;[16] *"through suffering shall you eat of it,"* meaning no longer will the land just produce—now it will require work to yield produce;[17] *"thorns and thistles shall it sprout"*—meaning when you plant, the earth shall bring forth plants that require preparation in order to be edible (prior, the food was readably edible);[18] *"you shall eat the herb,"* meaning you will be forced to eat herbs rather than the fruits of the garden.[19] Thus, the curse of the earth has a dramatic impact on plant life, and in particular, on trees.

Impact on Life

In summary, the Torah explains that approximately 100 million years ago there were only snakes with legs, and the earth had a particular Garden of Eden type of plant life. Then, sometime during the hour prior to the sin (i.e. between 100 Ma and 5771 years ago), snakes became abundant, and plant life on earth changed dramatically.

The scientific record agrees. The fossil record indicates that more than 100 million years ago there were no land snakes on earth, only lizards. Lizards have legs and are the animal that most closely resembles snakes. The fossil record for snakes is poor. The most widely accepted scientific theory suggests that snakes evolved from a family of lizards that lost their legs,[20] with modern snakes proliferating about 55 to 65 Ma.

During the same time frame the earth also experienced a significant extinction of plant life[21] and an extremely significant extinction of animal life (referred to as the Cretaceous–Tertiary [K/T] extinction event), most famously known for the extinction of the dinosaurs. Scientists theorize[22] the extinction event was caused by one or more catastrophic events (asteroid impact and/or volcanism), which triggered a domino effect; an absence of sunlight resulted in a major change in plant life, which caused the extinction of a number of plant-eating animals (those that could not adapt to the new kinds of plants), and consequently, resulted in the extinction of numerous carnivorous animals (those that could not adapt to the different sources of animal food).

Scientific and Torah descriptions of the extinction process agree that it started with a dramatic change in plant life. The Torah is clear that this change in plant life owed to the cursing of the ground. Scientists have concluded that this change was caused by an asteroid impact. Nothing in the Genesis narrative reveals whether or not God employed another natural event (like an asteroid impact) to accomplish the cursing of the ground.

The Torah narrative of the serpent's losing its legs and plant life having dramatically changed on earth leads to the same events recorded in the fossil record—a major extinction with a complete change in plant and animal life on earth and the emergence of snakes, a very successful and diversified species, all happening approximately 55-65 Ma, or about a half hour into the sin narrative.

Impact on Life from Adam's Fall Towards Sin: The First Four Extinction Events

The relationship between Adam's actions and the welfare of life on earth as described in specific instances in Genesis 2 and 3 (i.e. Adam prayed, it rained, and plants grew,[23] and Adam sinned and the earth was cursed[24]) are specific examples of a central and eternal relationship between humankind's actions and the well-being of life on earth. This relationship is explicitly described in Deuteronomy and is included in a central daily Jewish prayer (the Shema):

> It will be that if you hearken to My commandments...then I shall provide rain for your land in its proper time... I shall provide grass in your field for your cattle and you will eat...[25] Beware for yourselves, lest your heart be seduced and you turn astray... He will restrain the Heaven so there will be no rain, and the ground will not yield its produce... [26]

The above and other sections of the Torah are telling us that humans affect the weather and plant life, and can thus enhance or destroy life on earth via human actions (spiritual as well as physical).[27] Today, it is hard to assess the combined actions of humankind. However, during Day 6 the situation was clear: humankind was Adam and Eve, and every one of their negative actions affected the earth. These negative consequences on the planet's climate and plant life had a severe impact on animal life that must correspond with extinctions of life as recorded in the fossil record.

The sin of eating from the Tree of the Knowledge of Good and Bad, referred to as the primordial (original) sin in the rest of this chapter, turns out to be the end result of a number of lesser negative events. We first describe these negative events leading to the primordial sin of Adam, and then compare the timing of those events to the four major extinctions of life (in addition to the K/T extinction) on earth.[28]

As we shall see, angels play a role in this story. Thus, we digress to provide some background on angels. Do these supernatural beings really exist? Are they mentioned in Genesis? It turns out that angels go back as far as the Book of Genesis, where we read about angels calling out to Abraham at the binding of Isaac to stop the human sacrifice; angels appearing in Jacob's dream, Jacob wrestling with an angel; and there are many more accounts of angelic interactions with humans.

An angel[29] is a spiritual being without physical characteristics. The Hebrew word for angel is *malach*, which means messenger, for the angels are God's messengers sent to perform various missions. Every angel is programmed to perform certain tasks: The archangel Michael is dispatched on missions with expressions of God's kindness; Rafael's responsibility is to heal. Some angels are created for one specific task, and upon the task's completion they cease to exist. The angels were created on the second day,[30] and God consulted them when He decided to create humans on the sixth day.[31]

Thus angels play a key role in Scriptures, and as we shall see, on events leading to the primordial sin.

Events Leading to the Fall of Adam

The Sages teach, "*Envy, cupidity* [excessive desire] *and ambition* [or lack of humility and modesty] *remove man from the world* [i.e. cause him to sin]."[32] The Oral law goes on to elaborate that "*the three sins enumerated* [above] *brought about the* [primordial] *sin and punishment of Adam and Eve.*"[33]

The events leading to the primordial sin occurred in four steps. The first three steps were taken by Adam, and the last step by Adam and Eve. However, the angels played a major role in the first two steps.

Each step will be described and dated according to Genesis. These dates will then be compared to those established from the fossil record for extinction events. Timing of events on Day 6 is given by the hour. However, as will be seen, one can estimate the timing of events to partial hours. We use the following approximations: soon after (or before) the hour as 6 to 12 minutes after (or before) the hour, corresponding to 10 to 20 MY in Human Time (see Table 5.2), and halfway through the hour, or about 30 minutes into the hour, corresponding to 50 to 55 MY in Human Time.

Adam's Honor

As was discussed in greater detail in Chapter 5, Adam is pictured by most as a man like others today. However, this is not the case. Before the sin Adam was nothing like us physically or spiritually. After the sin he was greatly diminished and became closer to what we imagine.

In fact, before the sin the angels thought Adam was a deity: "*when he was created the angels erred* [thinking he was a divine being] *and wished to sing 'Holy' before him.*"[34] Taking this into account and the fact that ambition or indeed honor lead to sin, Rashi explains that "the honor which the Angels accorded to Adam led to his undoing."[35]

Adam is infused with his Godly soul in Hour 4 (see Figure 8.1), and was completed and stood up in Hour 5. The angels were partners in Adam's formation; thus, they must have realized Adam's greatness in the process of his creation and formation. This realization occurred after the infusion of the Godly soul and likely near the completion of Adam, or just before the end of Hour 5. The end of Hour 5 corresponds to 426 Ma (see Figure 8.1), and just before the end of Hour 5 corresponds to 436 to 446 Ma.

Envy of Adam

Once Adam is complete, the narrative tells us that vegetation begins to grow and Adam proceeds to name the animals. There is some difference of opinion in the commentaries as to when Adam enters the Garden of Eden: (i) after Hour 5 when the garden is being planted and made, or (ii) just before the sin when he is commanded not to eat. Clearly the animals that Adam was naming had to eat, so it's logical for the events of Hour 6 to occur in the Garden of Eden while the garden is developing. Rashi agrees since he states that God placed Adam in the garden before He put Adam into a deep sleep.[36] This deep sleep is part of the making of Eve in Hour 7; therefore, Adam was placed in the garden prior to this time. Once Adam is in the garden, the Oral Law tells us that *"the Angels envied the great honor and pleasure that Adam experienced in the Garden of Eden; and as a result they caused the Evil Inclination in the form of the snake to entice him."*[37]

This envy (downfall) event occurred during Hour 6, neither at the beginning nor the end, perhaps around the middle of the hour, or 370 to 375 Ma (see Figure 8.1), 426 Ma less about 50 to 55 MY.

Adam's Excessive Desire

While Adam assigned names to the animals, *"he did not find a helper corresponding to him."*[38] Hour 7 describes the formation of Eve as a mate for Adam. The text relates that Adam was put into a sleep and Eve was made from his side, and then (in a similar fashion to the animals) was brought to him.[39] At this point Adam, having dreamt about Eve during his sleep,[40] is unable to be patient due to his desire for her. "Adam and Eve were originally expected to wait until Shabbat [the end of Day 6] before engaging in marital relations. It is explained in Kabbalah that the essence of the sin was that they did not wait till the proper time to consummate their marriage."[41]

This excessive desire (downfall) event must occur once Eve is brought to Adam, most likely just past the middle of Hour 7, since the formation of Eve is an involved process. The middle of Hour 7 corresponds to about 265 Ma (see Figure 8.1), i.e., 320 Ma less 55 MY or more.

Adam and Eve's Immodesty

When Adam and Eve consummated their marriage, they did so in an immodest fashion, another step in the fall. "Had Eve merited, she would have epitomized the attribute of modesty... oblivious to the need for modesty as an acknowledgment of their essential, unknowable selves, their transcendent unity. She and Adam cohabited in the open; they were aware of being observed by the animals [see Babylonian Talmud, Niddah 17a]... Her [Eve ed.] fall continued with her immodest conversation with the snake..."[42]

After Eve is made in Hour 7, Cain and Abel are born in Hour 8. Thus, the *immodest* act above must start very early in Hour 8. The beginning of Hour 8 corresponds to 213 Ma (see Figure 8.1) and early in Hour 8 is therefore around 203 Ma (10 MY later).

Extinction Events Uncovered by Scientists

An extinction event is a sharp and large decrease in the diversity and abundance of macroscopic life. The fossil record shows a general background level of species becoming extinct as well as new ones appearing ever since macroscopic life began with the

Cambrian explosion. However, there are short periods where the extinctions are well above the general background level. It is generally agreed[43] that there have been five major extinction events, including the K/T event previously described.

Table 9.1 summarizes the events leading to the sin and compares their timing to the scientific estimates of the times for the four major extinction events (those other than the K/T event).

Table 9.1 Events Leading to Sin and Corresponding Major Extinctions

Creation Time	Creation event	Downfall event	Human Time	Science-derived Extinction event
Hour 5	Adam stood up	Adam's honor. Before the end of the hour.	436-446 Ma	Ordovician-Silurian 440-450 Ma
Hour 6	Adam entered the Garden	Adam's envy. The middle of the hour.	370-375 Ma	Late Devonian 360-375 Ma
Hour 7	Eve is brought to Adam	Adam's excessive desire. The middle of the hour.	After 265 Ma, well before 220 Ma	Permian-Triassic 251 Ma
Hour 8	Cain and Abel are born	Adam and Eve's immodesty. The beginning of the hour.	213- 203 Ma	Triassic-Jurassic 205 Ma

The evidence in the fossil record and the Genesis account are in nearly perfect agreement about the time of the mass extinctions. However, as with the appearance of life on earth, the descriptions provided by science and Genesis of the mechanism for these extinctions are different. Whereas scientists have concluded that past extinctions were due to natural events, the Torah links them to humankind's behavior. Today, humankind is probably causing significant extinctions through pollution, deforestation, and other consequences of human endeavor. These extinctions correlate to our physical actions on the planet; however, the Torah would argue they likewise owe to our straying from the Commandments (many of which would prohibit some of the physical actions taking place that have destructive consequences to planet earth).

We have seen that the time for appearances and mass extinctions of life derived from Genesis and observed in the fossil record correlate remarkably well. However, the story of life on earth will not be complete until we examine humankind in the next chapter.

---

[1] (i) David M. Raup and J. John Sepkoski Jr., "Mass Extinctions in the Marine Fossil Record," *Science*, v.215 No. 4539, 19 March 1982, pp.1501-1503.

(ii) John Alroy, "Dynamics of Origination and Extinction in the Marine Fossil Record," *The National Academy of Sciences of the USA*, 105 Supplement_1, (2008 August 12), pp.11536–11542.

[2] Paul D. Taylor, editor, *Extinctions in the History of Life* (Cambridge University Press, 2004).

[3] Arens, N. C., West, I. D., "Press-Pulse: A General Theory of Mass Extinction?" *Paleobiology* v. 34 (2008), p. 456.

[4] Michael Friedlander, *Pirkê de Rabbi Eliezer* [part of the oral law], (Illinois: Varda Books, 2004), p. 116.

[5] Genesis 3:1.

6   Genesis 3:14, Rashi explains "for the serpent originally had feet which were now removed."

7   Rabbi Meir Zlotowitz, Bereishis, *Genesis / A New Translation with a Commentary Anthologized from Talmudic Midrashic and Rabbinic Sources* (New York: Mesorah Publications Ltd., 1977), p. 114.

8   Genesis 3:4.

9   Numbers 22:28.

10   Ramban on Numbers 22:28.

11   Rabbi Meir Zlotowitz, Bereishis, *Genesis / A New Translation with a Commentary Anthologized from Talmudic Midrashic and Rabbinic Sources* (New York: Mesorah Publications Ltd., 1977), p. 114.

12   Genesis 3:11-13.

13   Genesis 3:17.

14   This can be illustrated with the following example. If a person goes mountain climbing at high altitude in the cold and does not properly protect his fingers, they immediately begin to freeze, become frostbitten, and later, fall off. The loss of fingers is a natural consequence of not taking action to protect them. The natural consequence is immediate; it begins right from the first moment the fingers are not protected, and completely manifests itself later with their loss. In a similar way, the natural consequence of the snake's action, loss of legs, sets in and develops over time, before the actual sin takes place.

15   Genesis 3:17.

16   Rabbi Meir Zlotowitz, Bereishis, *Genesis / A New Translation with a Commentary Anthologized from Talmudic Midrashic and Rabbinic Sources* (New York: Mesorah Publications Ltd., 1977), Ibn Ezra; Radak, p. 132.

[17]   Ibid. Midrash Aggadah; Radak, p. 133.

[18]   Ibid. Rashi, p. 133.

[19]   Ibid. Radak, p. 134.

[20]   Sebastián Apesteguía and Hussam Zaher, "A Cretaceous Terrestrial Snake with Robust Hind Limbs and a Sacrum," *Nature* 440 (20 April 2006), pp. 1037-1040. This article describes the newly discovered fossil of a snake that bears robust hind limbs and a sacral region that allowed the limbs to articulate with the backbone. This is probably the most primitive snake yet known, and its anatomy suggests a terrestrial, burrowing origin of snakes that originate from lizards.

[21]   (i) Peter Wilf and Kirk R. Johnson, "Land Plant Extinction at the End of the Cretaceous: A Quantitative Analysis of the North Dakota Megafloral Record," *Paleobiology* v.30 No.3 (September 2004), pp.347-368; explains that the K/T extinction is associated with the loss of nearly all dominant species, a significant drop in species richness, and no subsequent recovery. The loss of 1/3 to 3/5 of plant species supports a scenario of sudden ecosystem collapse.

(ii) Vivi Vajda, J. Ian Raine and Christopher J. Hollis, "Indication of Global Deforestation at the Cretaceous-Tertiary Boundary by New Zealand Fern Spike," *Science* v.294 No. 5547, 23 November 2001, pp. 1700–1702; explains that the devastating effect on terrestrial plant communities at the Cretaceous-Tertiary boundary was truly global.

[22]   Peter Schulte, *et al.*, "The Chicxulub Asteroid Impact and Mass Extinction at the Cretaceous-Paleogene Boundary," *Science* v.327 No. 5970, 5 March 2010, pp. 1214–1216.

[23]   Genesis 2:5.

[24]   Genesis 3:17.

[25]   Deuteronomy 11:13-15.

[26]   Deuteronomy 11:16,17.

[27]   The reason humankind has such an effect on the earth is that the earth was created for its sake. If humans do not earn God's blessings, there is no need for the rest of creation. Thus, humankind is to guard against losing the blessing of God. The earth's suffering is a natural consequence of humankind's actions. This relationship is illustrated by thinking of humankind as a bank executive and the earth as the bank. As the executive makes wrong decisions, the bank becomes weaker financially. At some point the executive goes too far, is brought to justice, and judged. Whatever punishment is given to the executive has little effect on the bank. The bank has long been in decline and its assets have been drained.

[28]   (i) David M. Raup and J. John Sepkoski Jr., "Mass Extinctions in the Marine Fossil Record," *Science*, v.215 No. 4539, 19 March 1982, pp.1501-1503.

(ii) John Alroy, "Dynamics of Origination and Extinction in the Marine Fossil Record," *The National Academy of Sciences of the USA*, 105 Supplement_1, (2008 August 12), pp. 11536–11542.

[29]   Ludwig Blau, Kaufmann Kohler, Angelology, 2002, Jewish Encyclopedia.com.

[30]   Michael Friedlander, *Pirkê de Rabbi Eliezer* (Illinois: Varda Books, 2004), Chapter 4.

[31]   (i) Targum Yonasan on Gen, 1:26, "And God said to the ministering Angels who had been created on the second day of the creation, 'Let us make man.' "

(ii) Genesis Midrash Rabbah 3:11.

[32]   Rabbi Moshe Lieber, *Ethics of our Fathers* (New York, Mesorah Publications Ltd, 2003) iv. 28,   bracketed words added by author.

[33]   Michael Friedlander, *Pirkê de Rabbi Eliezer* [part of the oral law], (Illinois: Varda Books, 2004), p.108, footnote 2.

[34]   Midrash, Rabbi Meir Zlotowitz, Bereishis, *Genesis / A New Translation with a Commentary Anthologized from Talmudic Midrashic and Rabbinic Sources* (New York, Mesorah Publications Ltd., 1977), p. 13.

[35]   Rabbi Moshe Lieber, *Ethics of our Fathers* (New York, Mesorah Publications Ltd, 2003), Footnotes to iv 28.

[36]   Rashi on Genesis 2:8.

[37]   Rabbi Moshe Lieber, *Ethics of our Fathers* (New York, Mesorah Publications Ltd, 2003), Footnotes to iv 28.

[38]   Genesis 2:20.

[39]   Genesis 2:21-23.

[40]   Genesis Rabbah 18:4.

[41]   Yitzchak Ginsburgh, *The Mystery of Marriage* (Israel: Gal Einai Publication Society, 1999), p. 315.

[42]   Yitzchak Ginsburgh, *The Mystery of Marriage* (Israel: Gal Einai Publication Society, 1999), pp. 394-395.

[43]   (i) David M. Raup and J. John Sepkoski Jr., "Mass Extinctions in the Marine Fossil Record," *Science*, v.215 No. 4539, 19 March 1982, pp.1501-1503.

       (ii) John Alroy, "Dynamics of Origination and Extinction in the Marine Fossil Record," *The National Academy of Sciences of the USA*, 105 Supplement_1, (2008 August 12), pp.11536–11542.

Chapter 10

Humankind

Where did our species come from?

When did humans appear on earth? And when did our species spread out across the planet?

Genesis provides a definitive answer to the first question. However, it does not provide details on the beginnings of humankind in general. The account moves on to relay information about the life of key characters (such as Cain and Noah) in order to provide moral teachings and spiritual insight.

Scientists, on the other hand, have studied these questions in detail and arrived at certain answers that continue to be refined and developed.

Humankind is, of course, a vast topic. This chapter provides only an outline of the Genesis account and a summary of scientific findings in order to illustrate areas of agreement and disagreement. Although we will describe the process by which humankind appears, as with the rest of the book, the focus is on the timeline of humankind's appearance.

The Genesis Perspective

We begin this chapter with Genesis and Adam. Adam was originally formed with both male and female characteristics (and later split into Adam and Eve) from two components: (1) a body *"formed of dust from the ground"*[1] (in similar fashion to the rest of the animals), and (2) *"a soul of life which was blown into his nostrils."*[2] As explained in Chapter 5, Adam was nothing like modern humans, physically or spiritually. And as shown in Chapter 8, Adam lived for hundreds of millions of years. Nonetheless, Genesis makes it very clear that we are descendants of Adam and Eve.

The Torah is also clear that as a consequence of the sin, Adam changed dramatically, both physically and spiritually, and became closer to what we are today. Pirkê de Rabbi Eliezer provides a vivid before-and-after description of Adam:

> *What was the dress of the first man? A skin of nail, and a cloud of glory covered him. When he ate of the fruits of the tree, the nail-skin was stripped off him, and the cloud of glory departed from him, and he saw himself naked... He curtailed his strength, and He shortened his stature... he was to sow wheat and to reap thistles, and his food was to be the grass of the earth, like that of the beast; and (he was to earn) his bread in anxiety, and his food by the sweat (of his brow); and after all these (curses came) death.*[3]

Despite the dramatic changes that Adam experienced, it was Eve who brought human death into the world. She was the first to eat from the fruit, and eating reaped the natural consequence of bringing death into the world, as it says in Genesis: *"the day you eat of it, you shall surely die."*[4] In fact, Eve's name (in Hebrew) was originally intended to be Chayah, which means "the living soul" and connotes eternal life. After she sinned, Adam called Eve "Chavah," which means "the mother of mortal life."[5] The Midrash explains how Eve brought about the consequence of death: *"It took tears and lamentations on her part to prevail upon Adam to take the step. Not yet being satisfied, she gave from the fruit to all living beings that they, too, might be subject to death."*[6]

Who were these other living beings? As we have seen in the creation timeline (refer to Figure 8.1), Adam and Eve had marital relations at least an hour prior to the sin, and conception and birth occurring prior to the sin was immediate and painless.[7] Not only did they give birth to Cain and Abel, but as the Rashi explains, they also gave birth to three girls, *"sisters,"* meaning perfect mates for Cain and Abel.[8] Beyond this first act of procreation, the text is clear that Adam and Eve are to start humanity and spread throughout the earth: *"be fruitful and multiply, fill the earth and subdue it..."*[9] This blessing is given to them before the sin,[10] and since a minute prior to the sin is equivalent to more than 1.5 million years, they had plenty of time to multiply and extend humanity through their offspring.

The next information on the progress of humankind provided in Genesis occurs in Chapter 4, right after the creation account, with the description of the occupations of Adam and Eve's first two children, Cain and Abel: *"Abel became a shepherd, and Cain became a tiller of the ground"*[11] and later *"he [Cain] became a city builder..."*[12] Thus, by 5,773 years ago, humankind had domesticated animals and was practicing agriculture and building cities.

In summary, the Genesis account states the following about humanity:

1. Humans are a special creation consisting of a body and a special Godly soul. Without this Godly soul humans would be like animals;

2. Humankind descended from a few individuals: Adam, Eve, and their children;

3. Procreation and production of humankind began prior to the sin; human death also commenced prior to the sin;

4. Before the sin, humans were told to spread throughout the earth and fill it; and

5. Finally, a more modern way of life, including agriculture, domesticated animals, and city dwelling, had begun by 5,773 years ago.

In addition, it should be noted that nothing in Genesis precludes the existence of human-like animals[13] with no Godly soul, existing and comprising other homo species.

The Scientific Perspective

What has scientific investigation revealed about the origins of humankind?

Scientific study of the fossil record has shown that the genus *Homo* (genus defined as a biological classification comprising a group of species) includes modern humans and species closely related to them, having appeared on earth from more than 2 million years ago. While the theory of evolution postulates that other *Homo* species might have been ancestors of *Homo sapiens* (modern humans); many were likely our "cousins," having evolved away from the *Homo sapiens* ancestral line. Today, we modern humans, known as *Homo sapiens*, are the only surviving *Homo* species, with other forms having become extinct over time, culminating with the extinction of Neanderthals 30,000 years ago.

Modern humans first appear in the fossil record in Africa about 195,000 years ago.[14] However, humans exhibiting what we would consider modern behavior, such as language, music, abstract thought, and a form of religious belief, appear perhaps around 50,000 years ago, and certainly by 10,000 years ago.[15]

The study of how humans populated the world has led to the now-accepted out-of-Africa theory.[16] The African exodus is estimated to have occurred about 60,000 to 100,000 years ago. Modern humans subsequently spread to all continents, replacing earlier *Homo* species, arriving in the Americas at least 14,500 years ago. Recent DNA studies[17] from people all over the world have revealed that humans today descend from a small group who lived in Africa. How small a group? Who knows? At this time there is no scientific consensus on the actual size of the group.

Excavations show that until 10,000 years ago, most humans lived as hunter-gatherers in small nomadic groups. The advent of agriculture led to the formation of permanent human settlements, the domestication of animals, and the use of metal tools. Agriculture encouraged trade and cooperation, and led to the formation of a complex society. About 6,000 years ago, the first proto-states developed in Mesopotamia, Egypt's Nile Valley, and the Indus Valleys. Military forces were formed for protection, and government bureaucracies for administration. States cooperated and competed for resources, in some cases waging wars.

In summary, scientific investigation has the following to say about human existence:

1. Humankind evolved from earlier species, with various *Homo* species coexisting for some time, but with only our species surviving today;

2. Humankind descended from a small group;

3. Humankind bearing an appearance consistent with ours today dates back to 195,000 years ago; however, humans exhibiting modern behavior are much more recent;

4. Humankind spread throughout the earth from Africa; and

5. About 6,000 years ago, our species settled into proto-states and undertook a more modern way of life.

In conclusion, setting aside the question of how modern humans emerged (either via creation or evolution; refer to the first point in the summaries above), the biblical and scientific accounts of what has happened since are consistent.

---

[1] Genesis 2:7.

[2] Ibid.

[3] Michael Friedlander, *Pirkê de Rabbi Eliezer* (Illinois: Varda Books, 2004), pp. 113-116.

[4] Genesis 2:17; Malbim's explanation.

⁵   Yitzchak Ginsburgh, *Parshat Chukat: Why Is There Death in the World?* Gal Einai Publication Society, pp. 1196-2208.

⁶   Rabbi Meir Zlotowitz, Bereishis, *Genesis / A New Translation with a Commentary Anthologized from Talmudic Midrashic and Rabbinic Sources* (New York, Mesorah Publications Ltd., 1977), Midrash, Genesis 3:7, p. 120.

⁷   Ibid. Midrash on Genesis 4:1, p. 141.

⁸   Ibid. Rashi on Genesis 4:2, p. 143.

⁹   Genesis 1:28.

¹⁰   (i) After Adam is created, we learn that he is to be "*fruitful and multiply, fill the earth* [start humanity]..." [Genesis 1:28]. The exact timing of this blessing is not provided by the Talmud reference on Day 6 [Babylonian Talmud, Sanhedrin 38b]. However, Genesis 2:25, the last sentence before the narrative on the sin, states "*they were naked, the man and his wife, and they were not ashamed.*" The commentary Sforno explains this means that they were cohabiting prior to the sin.

(ii) Michael Friedlander, *Pirkê de Rabbi Eliezer* [part of the oral law] (Illinois: Varda Books, 2004), Chapter 12: "The Holy One, blessed be He, made ten wedding canopies for Adam in the garden of Eden..." and "What is the custom observed by the precentor? He stands and blesses the bride in the midst of her wedding chamber. Likewise the Holy One, blessed be He, stood and blessed Adam and his help-mate, as it is said, 'And God blessed them...' (Genesis 1:28)." The preceding narrative makes it clear that they were blessed in the garden. The blessing was before the sin, since the narrative of the sin goes straight through to expulsion from the garden.

(iii) Genesis Rabbah 14: "The appearance of Adam and Eve, when just formed, was like that of persons of twenty years of age."

[11]   Genesis 4:2.

[12]   Genesis 4:17.

[13]   Gerald L. Schroeder, *The Science of God: the Convergence of Scientific and Biblical Wisdom* (New York: Broadway Books, 1997), Chapter 9.

[14]   Paul Mellars, "Why Did Modern Human Populations Disperse from Africa ca. 60,000 Years Ago?" *Proceedings of the National Academy of Sciences* v.103/25 (2006), pp. 9381-9386.

[15]   Sandra Scham, "The World's First Temple," *Archaeology* v.61 No. 6 (Nov/Dec 2008).

[16]   (i) Chris Stringer, "Human Evolution: Out of Ethiopia," *Nature* 423, pp. 692-695 (12 June 2003).

(ii) Gary Stix, "The Migration History of Humans: DNA Study Traces Human Origins Across the Continents," *Scientific American*, July 2008.

[17]   (i) Hillary Mayell, "Documentary Redraws Humans' Family Tree," *National Geographic News*, January 21, 2003.

(ii) R.L. Cann, M. Stoneking and A.C. Wilson, "Mitochondrial DNA and Human Evolution," *Nature* 325: 6099 (1987), pp.31-36.

Chapter 11

Conclusions

Did you know that God has different names?

What are they? What do they mean? And for that matter, isn't God's essence beyond any name? Yes, it certainly is.

As for His various names, these refer to the different ways in which He reveals Himself in creation. There are many names for God in the Bible.

What is a name? Do we think of ourselves or call ourselves by our given name? Not usually.

A name is a word, or specifically a title, by which the external world can refer to us. Over time our name becomes associated, by those who use it, with certain qualities or aspects of our personality, like kindness, honesty, or punctuality. Even finite beings like humans have many different names, such as dad, doctor, or teacher. Each of these emphasizes an aspect of our personality. God is infinite, yet He is referred to throughout the scriptures by many specific names. These names provide rich information as to what is happening in the Bible, since they tell us which aspect of God's essence is being revealed in a particular section of the text.

Let's examine some of His names, and then check which name is used in Genesis One, along with the information and clues that name conveys to us.

The Names of God

The names of God are so powerful that the Kabbalistic book Sefer Yetzirah (book of formation, attributed to Abraham) explains that the creation of the world was achieved by the manipulation of the sacred letters that form the Names of God. We also saw, in Chapter 4, that Isaac of Acre (the first to develop the time conversion factors) was an expert in composing the sacred names of God, by the power of which angels were forced to reveal to him the great mysteries.

In general, there are four categories of names ascribed to God.[1] We need only look at the two highest levels for the purpose of studying the creation narrative.

The first category is the essential name YHWH (pronounced Havayah), also called the Tetragrammaton, meaning the four-letter name. Havayah is the most sacred of God's names and comes closest to expressing His essence in certain contexts. Because of the special sanctity of the four-letter name YHWH, it is not pronounced today and was actually only pronounced within the Holy Temple in Jerusalem.

The second category contains those names that are sacred under Jewish law. Sacred means that a professional copyist of manuscripts (a scribe) must follow strict procedures when writing the Name. Once the scribe begins to write a name of God, he does not stop until it is finished. He must not be interrupted while writing it, even to greet a king. If an error is made in writing the Name, it may not be erased, but a line must be drawn around it to show that it is invalid, and the whole page must be put in a burial place for scripture, and then a new page is begun.

These sacred names are pronounced: Ekyeh (I will be), Kah, Kel, Elokah, Elokim, Tzevakot (Hosts), Shakai (Almighty), Adni (my Master), Akvah, and Ehevi. Each of these names has a specific meaning. The particular name being used reveals to us the role that God is assuming during a particular event in scripture.

For example,[2] the name Ekyeh is used in the book of Exodus. In this book God redeems the Jewish people from exile, which leads to their spiritual birth. Thus, the name Ekyeh implies new birth, or revelation of self. The name Shakai is used primarily in the book of Job, and signifies God's power to change the course of nature while remaining enclothed within it. It also signifies that he makes Himself consciously accessible to His creatures, regardless of their spiritual state. The name Elokim is the only name used in Genesis Chapter One, and thus we explore its meaning more fully below.

The Name Elokim

God's name Elokim corresponds to His property of strict judgment. Elokim creates nature through the act of apparent withdrawal or contraction of God's infinite light.[3] Elokim also can be translated as *"Master of all forces"*[4] and the *"Godly spirit of Law and Order."*[5] The use of Elokim indicates that the actions in the creation account are governed by strict law and order, and everything that occurred had to be based on cause and effect (as are occurrences in nature).

The parallel between Elokim and nature (haTeva in Hebrew) is further emphasized in Kabbalah. As we saw in Chapter 4, every Hebrew letter has a numerical value contributing to a total value for every word. Kabbalah teaches that if two words have the same numerical value, they are related. Elokim and nature have the same numerical value of 86. Thus, we conclude that Elokim is the revelation of the supernatural, as God appears in nature. God is manifest through this name, Elokim, as the inner essence of nature and its laws,[6] and God appears hidden within nature when the name Elokim is used.

Given that God is hidden within nature when he uses the name Elokim, as He does for all of Genesis One, we should not be surprised that the creation account can be well explained by science. Let's look at this concept in more detail below.

Genesis One and Nature

We have established in Chapters 6 through 9 that the Genesis[7] timeline and the science timeline are synchronized with regard to the formation of the universe and the appearance of life on earth.

Why is there such agreement between the supernatural, religion-based account, and scientific theory and observation? For the very reason that the supernatural remains mostly hidden or concealed within nature, and science describes nature.

The Genesis text uses two distinct words to describe God's actions: creation and formation. Creation is the divine act of making something out of nothing. Formation refers to taking something that already exists and making it into something else. The majority of the Genesis creation account describes formation events.

In Genesis One, God uses the name Elokim; therefore, His actions in the creation account are governed by strict law and order. Thus, we reason that what occurred in Genesis One was also based on cause and effect.

Consequently, any act of formation occurring in Genesis One should appear to us as something made from another substance naturally, by cause and effect. The acts of formation must be describable using the sciences of physics and biology, under the understanding of science as the study of naturally occurring phenomena based on cause and effect.

Any act of creation—making something from nothing—wherein the cause is supernatural should not be explainable by applying the scientific method, which by definition does not deal with explanations that are based on supernatural forces outside of nature. Thus, when Elokim uses a non-natural cause to create something from nothing, He reveals himself instead of remaining hidden within the law and order of nature, and what He creates cannot be fully explained by applying the scientific method.

Genesis One contains three such acts of creation where the cause is not natural: (1) the creation of the initial material of the universe at the beginning of the first day, (2) the creation of sea life on Day 5, and (3) the creation of man's spiritual component.

In addition, Genesis One contains one act of formation that is different from the rest. In general, formations are the acts of molding something into something else in a sequential progression. There is one exception: the formation of life. For life, the Genesis text emphasizes that each formation is of a different kind,[8] one not necessarily related to or formed from any other kind in an obvious way. As such, the formation of such a kind is beyond what science would describe as a naturally occurring sequential cause-and-effect process.

The vast majority of acts in the creation narrative are acts of formation by Elokim, the God of cause and effect. Studying acts of formation using the scientific method should thus produce accurate theories. However, there are three exceptions wherein the application of the scientific method should fail to yield complete explanations: (1) the beginning, (2) the first appearance of complex life (creation of sea creatures and the formation of each kind), and (3) the creation of man's spiritual part (his Godly soul). In these three instances, the cause is either supernatural or the act of formation is not sequential.

Scientists have (1) developed the Big Bang theory to explain cosmology, (2) developed the theory of evolution to grapple with the origins of life, and (3) dated and analyzed the fossil record to document the appearance of life on earth. The Big Bang theory is an excellent explanation of the development of the universe once a particular set of initial conditions are selected. As indicated in Chapter 3, scientists have difficulty explaining how the parameters at the beginning of the universe could have been so finely tuned that they ultimately led to the universe in which we live today. It is exactly at this point, the beginning of the universe, for which the scientific theory offers no satisfactory explanation; that the Genesis cosmological narrative elucidates a creation-from-nothing act.

Biologists and paleontologists struggle to explain certain key aspects of the fossil record: a long period of time between first microscopic life and complex life, the sudden appearance of very diverse life, and the subsequent appearance of additional life without a completely logical progression. In the words of Gould:

Three billion years of unicellularity, followed by five million years of intense creativity (the Cambrian explosion) and then capped by more than 500 million years of variation on set anatomical themes can scarcely be read as a predictable, inexorable or continuous trend toward progress or increasing complexity... We do not know why the Cambrian explosion could establish all major anatomical designs so quickly. [9]

It is not surprising that paleontologists and biologists are unable to completely explain these issues. Genesis clearly states that life was a creation from nothing in the oceans, that the first life forms were made at a specific time—coinciding with the Cambrian explosion—and that these life forms were specifically formed into different kinds.

Finally, the human race continues to grapple with humankind's special attributes. Application of the scientific method has shown how man's bodily design is similar to that of other animals (kinds), but it has not revealed from where certain modern behaviors and characteristics of the human species came. Genesis explains that a Godly soul, which gives humankind its particular characteristics, was infused as an out-of-nothing creation. The body, on the other hand, was formed in a process similar to that used to form the bodies of the animals.

Studying the formation of the universe and the appearance of life on earth via the scriptures and the scientific method using a code—the Genesis One code—in order to compare times and events provides us a unique perspective when pondering our origins. While science is able to greatly enrich the Genesis creation narrative with many wonderful details, insights, and natural laws, Genesis sheds light on events that science finds challenging by pointing out that these happen precisely when phenomena outside the putatively natural occurred.

The Zohar, which appeared about 800 years ago, prophesizes:

In the six hundredth year of the sixth [millennium], the gateways of heavenly wisdom and the fountains of lower wisdom will be opened, and the world will be uplifted to prepare for the ascension of the seventh [millennium]...[10]

The Lubavitcher Rebbe[11], expounding upon this verse in the Zohar, teaches:

Beginning from the year 5,600, or 1840 according to the secular calendar, the higher and lower waters opened. The lower waters are the wisdom of science. The higher waters are the wisdom of the Torah. The higher waters fertilize the lower waters, while the lower waters fertilize the higher waters. A great offspring will be born of the union of the two waters by the year 6,000 or 2240 according to the secular calendar, in time for the Messianic age.[12]

The Genesis creation narrative, interpreted with the aid of other biblical sources, describes events and times that match with those obtained from the best scientific theory and data currently available, a body of knowledge compiled primarily during the past 50 years.

What does this match mean to you?

My hope is that humankind's quest to know our origin can proceed from scientific theory and observation as well as from the Genesis creation narrative.

The End

---

[1]   Rabbi Yitzchak Ginsburgh, *What You Need to Know About Kabbalah* (New York, Dwelling Place Publishing Inc., 2006).

---

[2] Rabbi Yitzchak Ginsburgh, *The Names of God: Eleven Holy Names of God Associated with the Sefirot*, Gal Einai Institute (2004).

[3] Ibid.

[4] Ramban on Genesis 1:3.

[5] H. Moose, *In the Beginning: The Bible Unauthorized* (California: Thirty Seven Books, 2001), Genesis 1.

[6] Yitzchak Ginsburgh, *The Mystery of Marriage* (Israel: Gal Einai Publication Society, 1999), p. 424.

[7] Herein, referring to Genesis chapters 1 to 3.

[8] Rabbi Meir Zlotowitz, Bereishis, *Genesis / A New Translation with a Commentary Anthologized from Talmudic Midrashic and Rabbinic Sources* (New York: Mesorah Publications Ltd., 1977), Genesis 1:22, p. 66.

[9] Stephen Jay Gould, "The Evolution of Life on Earth," *Scientific American*, October 1994, pp. 85-91.

[10] Zohar I, 117a.

[11] Menachem Mendel Schneerson (April 5, 1902–June 12, 1994), known as the Lubavitcher Rebbe among his followers, was a prominent Hasidic rabbi and the seventh and last Rebbe (Hasidic leader) of the Chabad-Lubavitch. Chabad-Lubavitch is a branch of Orthodox Judaism that promotes spirituality and joy through the popularization and internalization of Jewish mysticism as the fundamental aspects of the Jewish faith movement.

[12] Rabbi Yitzchak Ginsburgh, *The Higher and Lower Waters: Incorporating Art and Science into Torah Education*, Gal Einai Institute (1996-2008).

Annex A

Genesis (King James Version)

Genesis 1

1   In the beginning God created the heaven and the earth.

2   And the earth was without form, and void; and darkness was upon the face of the deep. And the Spirit of God moved upon the face of the waters.

3   And God said, Let there be light: and there was light.

4   And God saw the light, that it was good: and God divided the light from the darkness.

5   And God called the light Day, and the darkness he called Night. And the evening and the morning were the first day.

6   And God said, Let there be a firmament in the midst of the waters, and let it divide the waters from the waters.

7   And God made the firmament, and divided the waters which were under the firmament from the waters which were above the firmament: and it was so.

8   And God called the firmament Heaven. And the evening and the morning were the second day.

9   And God said, Let the waters under the heaven be gathered together unto one place, and let the dry land appear: and it was so.

10   And God called the dry land earth; and the gathering together of the waters He called Seas: and God saw that it was good.

11   And God said, Let the earth bring forth grass, the herb yielding seed, and the fruit tree yielding fruit after his kind, whose seed is in itself, upon the earth: and it was so.

12   And the earth brought forth grass, and herb yielding seed after his kind, and the tree yielding fruit, whose seed was in itself, after his kind: and God saw that it was good.

[13] And the evening and the morning were the third day.

[14] And God said, Let there be lights in the firmament of the heaven to divide the day from the night; and let them be for signs, and for seasons, and for days, and years:

[15] And let them be for lights in the firmament of the heaven to give light upon the earth: and it was so.

[16] And God made two great lights; the greater light to rule the day, and the lesser light to rule the night: he made the stars also.

[17] And God set them in the firmament of the heaven to give light upon the earth,

[18] And to rule over the day and over the night, and to divide the light from the darkness: and God saw that it was good.

[19] And the evening and the morning were the fourth day.

[20] And God said, Let the waters bring forth abundantly the moving creature that hath life, and fowl that may fly above the earth in the open firmament of heaven.

[21] And God created great whales, and every living creature that moveth, which the waters brought forth abundantly, after their kind, and every winged fowl after his kind: and God saw that it was good.

[22] And God blessed them, saying, Be fruitful, and multiply, and fill the waters in the seas, and let fowl multiply in the earth.

[23] And the evening and the morning were the fifth day.

[24] And God said, Let the earth bring forth the living creature after his kind, cattle, and creeping thing, and beast of the earth after his kind: and it was so.

[25] And God made the beast of the earth after his kind, and cattle after their kind, and every thing that creepeth upon the earth after his kind: and God saw that it was good.

[26] And God said, Let us make man in our image, after our likeness: and let them have dominion over the fish of the sea, and over the fowl of the air, and over the cattle, and over all the earth, and over every creeping thing that creepeth upon the earth.

[27] So God created man in his own image, in the image of God created he him; male and female created he them.

[28] And God blessed them, and God said unto them, Be fruitful, and multiply, and replenish the earth, and subdue it: and have dominion over the fish of the sea, and over the fowl of the air, and over every living thing that moveth upon the earth.

[29] And God said, Behold, I have given you every herb bearing seed, which is upon the face of all the earth, and every tree, in the which is the fruit of a tree yielding seed; to you it shall be for meat.

[30] And to every beast of the earth, and to every fowl of the air, and to everything that creepeth upon the earth, wherein there is life, I have given every green herb for meat: and it was so.

[31] And God saw everything that he had made, and, behold, it was very good. And the evening and the morning were the sixth day.

Genesis 2

[1] Thus the heavens and the earth were finished, and all the host of them.

[2] And on the seventh day God ended his work which he had made; and he rested on the seventh day from all his work which he had made.

[3] And God blessed the seventh day, and sanctified it: because that in it he had rested from all his work which God created and made.

[4] These are the generations of the heavens and of the earth when they were created, in the day that the LORD God made the earth and the heavens,

[5] And every plant of the field before it was in the earth, and every herb of the field before it grew: for the LORD God had not caused it to rain upon the earth, and there was not a man to till the ground.

[6] But there went up a mist from the earth, and watered the whole face of the ground.

⁷ And the LORD God formed man of the dust of the ground, and breathed into his nostrils the breath of life; and man became a living soul.

⁸ And the LORD God planted a garden eastward in Eden; and there he put the man whom he had formed.

⁹ And out of the ground made the LORD God to grow every tree that is pleasant to the sight, and good for food; the tree of life also in the midst of the garden, and the tree of knowledge of good and evil.

¹⁰ And a river went out of Eden to water the garden; and from thence it was parted, and became into four heads.

¹¹ The name of the first is Pison: that is it which compasseth the whole land of Havilah, where there is gold;

¹² And the gold of that land is good: there is bdellium and the onyx stone.

¹³ And the name of the second river is Gihon: the same is it that compasseth the whole land of Ethiopia.

¹⁴ And the name of the third river is Hiddekel: that is it which goeth toward the east of Assyria. And the fourth river is Euphrates.

¹⁵ And the LORD God took the man, and put him into the garden of Eden to dress it and to keep it.

¹⁶ And the LORD God commanded the man, saying, Of every tree of the garden thou mayest freely eat:

¹⁷ But of the tree of the knowledge of good and evil, thou shalt not eat of it: for in the day that thou eatest thereof thou shalt surely die.

¹⁸ And the LORD God said, It is not good that the man should be alone; I will make him an help meet for him.

¹⁹ And out of the ground the LORD God formed every beast of the field, and every fowl of the air; and brought them unto Adam to see what he would call them: and whatsoever Adam called every living creature, that was the name thereof.

[20] And Adam gave names to all cattle, and to the fowl of the air, and to every beast of the field; but for Adam there was not found an help meet for him.

[21] And the LORD God caused a deep sleep to fall upon Adam, and he slept: and he took one of his ribs, and closed up the flesh instead thereof;

[22] And the rib, which the LORD God had taken from man, made he a woman, and brought her unto the man.

[23] And Adam said, This is now bone of my bones, and flesh of my flesh: she shall be called Woman, because she was taken out of Man.

[24] Therefore shall a man leave his father and his mother, and shall cleave unto his wife: and they shall be one flesh.

[25] And they were both naked, the man and his wife, and were not ashamed.

Genesis 3

[1] Now the serpent was more subtil than any beast of the field which the LORD God had made. And he said unto the woman, Yea, hath God said, Ye shall not eat of every tree of the garden?

[2] And the woman said unto the serpent, We may eat of the fruit of the trees of the garden:

[3] But of the fruit of the tree which is in the midst of the garden, God hath said, Ye shall not eat of it, neither shall ye touch it, lest ye die.

[4] And the serpent said unto the woman, Ye shall not surely die:

[5] For God doth know that in the day ye eat thereof, then your eyes shall be opened, and ye shall be as gods, knowing good and evil.

[6] And when the woman saw that the tree was good for food, and that it was pleasant to the eyes, and a tree to be desired to make one wise, she took of the fruit thereof, and did eat, and gave also unto her husband with her; and he did eat.

[7] And the eyes of them both were opened, and they knew that they were naked; and they sewed fig leaves together, and made themselves aprons.

[8] And they heard the voice of the LORD God walking in the garden in the cool of the day: and Adam and his wife hid themselves from the presence of the LORD God amongst the trees of the garden.

[9] And the LORD God called unto Adam, and said unto him, Where art thou?

[10] And he said, I heard thy voice in the garden, and I was afraid, because I was naked; and I hid myself.

[11] And he said, Who told thee that thou wast naked? Hast thou eaten of the tree, whereof I commanded thee that thou shouldest not eat?

[12] And the man said, The woman whom thou gavest to be with me, she gave me of the tree, and I did eat.

[13] And the LORD God said unto the woman, What is this that thou hast done? And the woman said, The serpent beguiled me, and I did eat.

[14] And the LORD God said unto the serpent, Because thou hast done this, thou art cursed above all cattle, and above every beast of the field; upon thy belly shalt thou go, and dust shalt thou eat all the days of thy life:

[15] And I will put enmity between thee and the woman, and between thy seed and her seed; it shall bruise thy head, and thou shalt bruise his heel.

[16] Unto the woman he said, I will greatly multiply thy sorrow and thy conception; in sorrow thou shalt bring forth children; and thy desire shall be to thy husband, and he shall rule over thee.

[17] And unto Adam he said, Because thou hast hearkened unto the voice of thy wife, and hast eaten of the tree, of which I commanded thee, saying, Thou shalt not eat of it: cursed is the ground for thy sake; in sorrow shalt thou eat of it all the days of thy life;

[18] Thorns also and thistles shall it bring forth to thee; and thou shalt eat the herb of the field;

[19] In the sweat of thy face shalt thou eat bread, till thou return unto the ground; for out of it wast thou taken: for dust thou art, and unto dust shalt thou return.

[20] And Adam called his wife's name Eve; because she was the mother of all living.

[21] Unto Adam also and to his wife did the LORD God make coats of skins, and clothed them.

[22] And the LORD God said, Behold, the man is become as one of us, to know good and evil: and now, lest he put forth his hand, and take also of the tree of life, and eat, and live forever:

[23] Therefore the LORD God sent him forth from the garden of Eden, to till the ground from whence he was taken.

[24] So he drove out the man; and he placed at the east of the garden of Eden Cherubims, and a flaming sword which turned every way, to keep the way of the tree of life.

Annex B

Divine Time

Divine Time is the fundamental inner working clock of the universe.

In this section we explore mystical works to arrive at an understanding of Divine Time and the relation between the Creation and Divine timelines. To determine Divine Time, one must first understand the central roles of numbers 7 and 49 in biblical literature, and the concept of sabbatical cycles.

Cycles of 7 and 49

The numbers 7 and 49 are crucial in the Torah. Seven signifies completion of a fundamental process, e.g., the week. Forty-nine signifies the completion of seven cycles of seven, usually associated with more fundamental or final completion. These cycles involving 49 appear as complete spiritual, agricultural, and cosmic cycles. The first two are described in direct biblical sources; the later cycles (cosmic) are derived from Kabbalistic interpretation of a Talmudic source.

Spiritual Cycles – the Counting of the Omer

The Counting of the Omer is a verbal counting of each of the 49 days between the Jewish holidays of Passover, the holiday celebrating the exodus from Egypt, and Shavuot, the holiday celebrating the giving of the Torah. This commandment begins the day on which the Omer, a sacrifice containing an omer-measure (an ancient Hebrew measure corresponding to approximately 3.5 liters) of barley was offered in the Temple in Jerusalem, and ends the day before an offering of wheat was brought to the Temple on Shavuot. The Counting of the Omer begins on the second day of Passover and ends the day before the holiday of Shavuot.

The commandment for counting the Omer is recorded in Leviticus:[1]

> *You shall count for yourselves—from the morrow of the rest day, from the day when you bring the omer of the waving—seven weeks, they shall be complete. Until the morrow of the seventh week you shall count, fifty days; and you shall offer a new meal-offering to God.*

The idea of counting each day represents spiritual preparation and anticipation for the receiving of the Torah. The period of the Omer is considered to be a time of potential inner growth, a time for one to further improve positive characteristics through reflection, and to further develop one trait on each of the 49 days.

Thus, spiritually, there are seven cycles of seven weeks with a complete spiritual cycle being 49 days.

Physical Cycles – Sabbatical Cycles for the Land

Shmita (literally release), also called the Sabbatical Year, is the seventh year of the seven-year agricultural cycle mandated by the Torah for the Land of Israel. During Shmita, the land is left to lie fallow and all agricultural activity—including plowing, planting, pruning, and harvesting—is forbidden by Torah law.[2]

> *For six years you may sow your field, and for six years you may prune your vineyard; and you may gather in its crops. But the seventh year shall be a complete rest for the land, a Sabbath for God…it shall be a year of rest for the land.*

The idea of the seventh rest year is also connected with debt. In the seventh year every creditor shall remit any debt owed by his neighbor and brother.[3]

At the end of seven years you shall institute a remission. This is the matter of the remission. Every creditor shall remit his authority over what he has lent to his fellow; he shall not press his fellow or his brother; for He has proclaimed a remission for God.

After seven such sabbatical cycles, i.e., 49 years, comes the Jubilee, or the ultimate completion. The Jubilee year is the year at the end of seven cycles of Sabbatical years, and according to Torah regulations it had a special impact on land ownership and management in the territory of the kingdoms of Israel and of Judah.[4]

And you shall count for yourself seven cycles of sabbatical years, seven years seven times; the years of the seven cycles of sabbatical years shall be for you forty-nine years....You shall sanctify the fiftieth year and proclaim freedom throughout the land for all its inhabitants; it shall be the jubilee year for you; you shall return each man to his ancestral heritage and you shall return each man to his family.

The Torah further states:[5] *"The land shall not be sold in perpetuity, for the land is Mine [God's], for you are sojourners and residents with Me."* The land can be sold only for the number of crops it will yield until the Jubilee year, when it reverts to its original owner. Thus, the Jubilee year existed because the land was the possession of God, and its current occupiers were merely tenants. Therefore, the land shouldn't be sold forever.

Cosmic Cycles – 49,000 Years[6]

One of the more controversial teachings among Kabbalists is the doctrine of the Shmita applied cosmically.

Among the earlier generations of Kabbalists, prior to the Arizal, many wrote about the doctrine of the Shmita, including the Arizal's teacher, Rabbi David Ibn Zimra. These Kabbalists taught that not only is the doctrinal source of the Shmita to be found in the Oral Tradition, but also they made use of the plain words of the Torah text to show that the history of time is not fully told in the Torah alone.

As shown above, it is written in the book of Leviticus that for six years fields are to be sown, and for the seventh, the land is to be allowed to rest.[7] It is also taught by the Sages in the Talmud:[8] "*Six thousand years shall the world exist, and one [one thousand, the seventh], it shall be desolate.*" Kabbalists learned from the secret meaning of the verse in Leviticus that the days of our world will be measured in the same way as the biblical Sabbatical year. Six years shall we labor, and in the seventh shall we rest. So, our civilization will grow for 6,000 years, and then for 1,000 years shall it remain desolate, which means left alone to rest.

We are instructed to count seven times seven years and then to proclaim a Jubilee, a year of complete release. The Kabbalists have revealed that just as our civilization will last for the Sabbatical period of 6,000 years and 1,000 years of desolation, so will there be seven cycles similar to this, corresponding to a cosmic cycle of Sabbatical years totaling 49,000 years.

Thus, biblical completion of spiritual and agricultural full cycles is 49 days and years respectively. Cosmically, the equivalent is 49,000 years, at which point the physical universe returns to its original owner.

The Divine Timeline

The concept of Divine Time and cosmic cycles has been developed and explained by Rabbi Kaplan[9] and clarified by Rabbi Ari D. Kahn.[10] This section further develops the divine timeline and plots it in parallel to the creation timeline.

In the 13th century, Rabbi Isaac of Acre, in his work *Otzar HaChaim* (Life's Treasure),[11] agreed with the concept that the universe will exist for 49,000 years. His was the first work to teach that since Sabbatical cycles existed before man was created, time before Adam and Eve must be measured in divine years (where, as we saw earlier, one Divine day is 1,000 years of Human Time[12]). Rabbi Isaac of Acre was thus the first to see that the universe is billions of years old. Rabbi Kaplan in his interpretation of Rabbi Isaac of Acre's work assumes that we are currently in the seventh sabbatical cycle. This is a controversial teaching, since most Kabbalists teach that we are in the second cycle.

The work described above has placed the occurrence of earlier cosmic cycles prior to the Genesis narrative. This author hypothesizes the following:

1. the cycles start with the beginning of the universe as we know it , with Day 1 in the Genesis narrative),

2. a creation day is an epoch of time,

3. the universe will exist for seven cycles, or 49,000 years, and

4. the current cycle is the last 7,000-year cycle, or seventh cycle, as we approach the messianic era.

Therefore, each of the six creation days is 7,000 years, one cycle, and we are now in the last 7,000 years of the existence of the universe as we know it, or the seventh cycle.

The above result is inspired by the controversial concept of cosmic cycles. However, more recent Kabbalistic works support the 7,000-years-per-creation-day approach and thus lead to the same result. Rabbi Isaac Luria, the Arizal, does not support the concept of cosmic sabbatical cycles. The book *Etz Chaim* is a classic of Rabbi Isaac Luria's School of Kabbalah. Rabbi Salman Eliyahu, in his book *Kerem Shlomo on Etz Chaim* (a commentary on Etz Chaim), asserts that if something is perfected and complete, it has gone through a whole 7,000-year cycle. Each of the creation days was perfected, rectified, and pure, and had gone through its own 7,000-year completion; thus, each creation day represents 7,000 years.[13]

Given the above, Divine Time proceeds in periods of 7,000 years. As illustrated in Table B.1 below, each of the first six days of creation corresponds to 7,000 divine years: Day 1, from 0 to 7,000; Day 2, from 7,000 to 14,000; and so on, until Day 6, from 35,000 to 42,000. Following Day 6, from year 42,000 to 49,000, Divine Time corresponds to the 6,000 years of the Jewish calendar followed by the 1,000 years of the seventh millennium.

Table B.1 Seven Sabbatical Cycles

Creation Time	Day 1	Day 2	Day 3	Day 4	Day 5	Day 6	7,000 years*
Sabbatical Cycle	1st Cycle	2nd Cycle	3rd Cycle	4th Cycle	5th Cycle	6th Cycle	7th Cycle
Divine Years	7,000	7,000	7,000	7,000	7,000	7,000	7,000
Divine Time	0–7,000	7,000–14,000	14,000–21,000	21,000–28,000	28,000–35,000	35,000–42,000	42,000–49,000
*7,000 years = 6,000 years of the biblical calendar + 1,000 years of the seventh millennium							

Figure B.1 depicts the creation timeline for Day 6 and the parallel divine timeline.

Divine Time (thousands of years)	Creation Time	DAY 6 (hours)	Creation Events
38500		12	
38792		1	Dust was gathered
39083	974 generations before Adam	2	Dust kneaded into shapeless mess; Formation of complex life begins
39375		3	Adam's limbs shaped
39667		4	Soul infused into Adam
39958		5	Adam rose and stood on his feet
40250		6	Adam named the animals
40542		7	Eve was created
40833		8	Cain and Abel born. Garden is planted after man created.
41125		9	Adam and Eve are commanded to not eat from the Tree
41417		10	Adam and Eve sinned
41708		11	Adam and Eve were tried
42000		12	Adam and Eve were expelled from the Garden

Figure B.1 Creation Time and Divine Time – Day 6

The "Birth" of Adam in Divine Time

The Talmud states "nine hundred and seventy-four generations pressed themselves forward to be created before the world was created, but were not created: the Holy One, blessed be He, arose and planted them in every generation."[14] This is also derived from the verse "The word which He commanded to a thousand generations,"[15] which, according to Rashi, means that the Torah was given, not for 1,000 generations, but to the 1,000th generation. By subtracting from 1,000 the 26 generations between Adam and Moses (who was given the Torah), we likewise obtain 974.

The Torah either gives us exact time for a generation by spelling out the dates when people were born and died (as for the generations between Adam and Moses), or in the absence of details, assumes a generation is 40 years. This is most famously expressed as "The wrath of God burned against Israel and He made them wander in the Wilderness for forty years, until the end of the entire generation…"[16] To calculate the time in Divine Time from the beginning to the end of the intended 974th generation, one multiplies 974 by 40 to obtain 38,960 years. Converting this to the time on the creation timeline (dividing 38,960 by 7,000), we arrive at 1.577 hours into Day 6, i.e., 34.6 minutes into the second hour (see Figure B.1). This is the hour of which it is said, "God kneaded the dust into a shapeless mass," i.e., began to form Adam. This analysis shows that Adam was "born" precisely after the intended 974th generation, in the divine year 38,960, which further supports using 7,000 years per creation day to derive the divine timeline. (Please note that commentaries[17] on the Talmud verse quoted in the preceding paragraph place the intended 974 generations prior to Day 1, or prior to *"let there be light"*; thus, there is no commentary that justifies or supports the above calculation.)[18]

---

[1]   Leviticus 23:15-16.

---

[2] Leviticus 25:3-5.

[3] Deuteronomy 15:1-3.

[4] Leviticus 25:8-13.

[5] Leviticus 25:23 and commentary footnote.

[6] Aryeh Kaplan, Yaakov Elman, and Israel ben Gedaliah Lipschutz, *Immortality, Resurrection, and the Age of the Universe: A Kabbalistic View* (Israel: Ktav Publishing House, January 1993), pp. 6-9.

[7] Leviticus 25:3-5.

[8] Babylonian Talmud, Sanhedrin 97a.

[9] Rabbi Aryeh Kaplan, *The Age of the Universe: A Torah True Perspective* (Rueven Meir Caplan, 2008).

[10] Rabbi Ari D. Kahn, *Explorations* (Israel: Targum Press, 2001), parshat Bahr.

[11] Rabbi Isaac of Acre, *Otzar HaChaim (Life's Treasure)*, Guenz-berg collection, Lenin Library, Moscow. Also Rabbi Aryeh Kaplan, *The Age of the Universe: A Torah True Perspective* (Rueven Meir Caplan, 2008), p. 17.

[12] *"For a thousand years in your sight are but like yesterday when it is past"* (Psalm 90:4), as interpreted in the Babylonian Talmud, Sanhedrin 97a and 97b.

[13] Yitzchak Ginsburgh, *The Shemitot and the Age of the Universe*, Gal Einai Publication Society, February 2011, part 3.

[14] Babylonian Talmud, Hagigah 13b, 14a.

[15] Psalm 105:8.

[16] Numbers 32:1.

[17] Yitzchak Ginsburgh, *The Shemitot and the Age of the Universe*, Gal Einai Publication Society, February 2011, part 3.

[18]   It is interesting to note that it took three hours to form Adam to the point when he receives the Godly soul. Since Adam is the father of humankind, and it takes 40 weeks to form a baby during pregnancy, these three hours of Adam's formation parallel the 40 weeks of pregnancy. Thus, 34.6 minutes into the three hours equates to the 54th day of pregnancy. Counting from conception (as the Talmud does, rather than from the last menstrual cycle), the 34.6 minutes equate to the 40th day of pregnancy. The Talmud says an embryo is considered unformed for the first 40 days and cannot be regarded as a fetus until after the 40th day (Babylonian Talmud, Yebamoth 69b); similarly, Adam became the equivalent of a "fetus" halfway through the second hour, when his generation started.

Glossary

A priori: made before or without examination; not supported by factual study.

Adam: the first created man. He looked nothing like us. Only after his sin was he diminished, thereby becoming more like us. Normal humans are referred to as humankind. Adam is referred to as Adam or man.

Angel: a spiritual being without physical characteristics; a messenger sent by God to perform certain tasks (*malach* in Hebrew).

Background extinction rate: average rate at which species have become extinct over the past 550 million years (not including recent human-caused extinction).

BCE: before the Common Era; covers the time prior to Christ's birth.

BY: billion years.

Cambrian explosion: the relatively rapid appearance of complex animals approximately 530 million years ago, as found in the fossil record.

Christian Right: a term used predominantly in the United States to describe a spectrum of right-wing Christian political and social movements and organizations characterized by their strong support of conservative social and political values.

Commentaries: critical explanations or interpretations of the Biblical texts.

Concordance model: the best-fitting set of cosmological parameters, i.e. those that produce the best match between theory and observation.

Cosmological parameters: parameters that define the properties of the universe and are the main input to the Big Bang model.

Cosmology: the study of how the universe began and developed.

Counting of the Omer: a verbal counting of each of the 49 days between the Jewish holidays of Passover (the holiday celebrating the exodus from Egypt) and Shavuot (the holiday celebrating the giving of the Torah).

Creation day: 2.54 billion years in Human Time, or 7,000 years in Divine Time.

Creation Time: time as per the six-day creation account in Genesis.

Creation timeline: the six-day chronological account of the creation of the universe and life in Genesis.

Creation: the divine act of making something out of nothing.

Creation-evolution controversy: also known as the origins debate; a recurring cultural, political and theological dispute about the origins of the earth, humanity, life and the universe. The dispute is among those who espouse religious belief and thus support a creationist view versus those who accept evolution as supported by scientific consensus.

Cretaceous Period: from 135 million to 63 million years ago; end of the age of reptiles; appearance of modern insects and flowering plants.

Divine day: 1,000 years of Human Time.

Divine Time: time as kept by God. One divine day is 1,000 years in human terms (Human Time).

Elokim: The name of God used in Genesis One, indicating that the actions in the creation account are governed by strict law and order and everything that occurred had to be based on cause and effect.

Epoch interpretation: an interpretation of the six days in the creation narrative as six epochs or eras.

Eugenics: the study of hereditary improvement of the human race by controlled selective breeding.

Eve: the first woman. After she sinned Adam called her Chavah, which means the mother of mortal life.

Extinction events: or mass extinctions; denotes large extinctions that have occurred over a relatively short period of time, during which the number of species that went extinct was significantly higher than that to be expected (five have occurred since life began).

Extinction: the end of an organism or group of organisms, typically a species.

Fine tuning problem: the problem that arises when one varies almost any of the particular properties of the universe, the laws of physics and their parameters by a very modest amount, with the variation leading to circumstances whereby the universe cannot exist.

Formation: the act of taking something that already exists and making it into something else.

Fossils: the preserved remains or traces of animals, plants, and other organisms from the remote past.

Genetics: the branch of biology that deals with heredity, especially the mechanisms of hereditary transmission and the variation of inherited characteristics among similar or related organisms.

Genus: A taxonomic category ranking below a family and above a species, and generally consisting of a group of species.

Half-life: the time required for something to fall to half its initial value; in this work's context, the time for half the atoms in a radioactive substance to decay.

Homo: genus that includes modern humans and species closely related to them.

Human Time: time as kept by human beings.

Intelligent design: the proposition that certain features of the universe and of living things are best explained by an intelligent cause, not an undirected process such as natural selection.

Isaac ben Samuel of Acre (fl. 13th-14th centuries): a Kabbalist who lived in the Land of Israel; author of Otzar HaChaim.
Isotope: one of two or more atoms with the same atomic number (number of protons) but with different numbers of neutrons.

It was good: phrase meaning "completed to the point that it was useful to man."

It was so: phrase meaning "became eternally established."

Jubilee year: the year at the end of seven cycles of Sabbatical years (see Shmita), which, according to Torah regulations, had a special impact on the ownership and management of land in the territory of the kingdoms of Israel and of Judah.

Kabbalah: receiving or tradition; a discipline and school of thought concerned with the mystical aspect of Judaism.

Kind: unit of life that is formed or created as described in Genesis; interpreted to correspond to a species.

Kingdom: the second highest rank in a taxonomic classification, containing at least six subdivisions.

Last universal ancestor: term for the hypothetical single-cellular organism or the single cell from which all organisms now living on earth descended.

Life: matter characterized by the ability to metabolize nutrients, grow, reproduce, and respond and adapt to environmental stimuli.

Louisiana Balanced Treatment Act: act passed in 1981 in the U.S. state of Louisiana that required schools to provide balanced treatment of creation and evolutionary science.

Ma: million years ago.

Maimonides: a pre-eminent Jewish philosopher and one of the greatest Torah scholars of the Middle Ages.

Mass extinction event: see Extinction events.

Mercy: the first of the emotive attributes of the Sefirot. It is the desire to give without limitation; corresponds to the biological classification level of phylum.

Midrash: meaning exposition; denotes non-legalistic teachings of the rabbis of the Talmudic era.

Midrash Rabbah: a Midrah dedicated to explaining the five books of Moses.

Milky Way: galaxy containing our solar system and consisting of a central older bulge and a younger disk where the solar system formed.

Modern Humans: our species, *Homo sapiens.*

MY: million years.

Names of God: different names that refer to various ways in which He reveals Himself in creation.

Nebular hypothesis: model explaining the formation and evolution of the solar system. A precursor of the Big Bang at the solar-system level.

Neo-Darwinian synthesis: maintains that evolution is a purely materialistic process driven by the natural selection of random variation at the genetic level.

Nucleosynthesis: the process by which heavier chemical elements are synthesized from hydrogen nuclei in the interiors of stars.

Old earth creationism: umbrella term for a number of creationism concepts. The worldview of proponents is typically more compatible with mainstream scientific thought on the issues of geology, cosmology, and the age of the earth. Some proponents interpret the six days of creation as six epochs.

Omer: a sacrifice containing an omer-measure (an ancient Hebrew measure corresponding to approximately 3.5 liters).

Oral Law: used to interpret and apply the Written Law. It is now documented in writing. It consists primarily of the Talmud, Explanations, Midrashim and Zohar.

Organic evolution: the sequence of events involved in the evolutionary development of a species or related group of organisms.

Origins debate: see Creation–evolution controversy.

Otzar HaChaim: Kabbalistic work by Isaac ben Samuel. Was the first work to state that the universe is actually billions of years old; Isaac arrived at this conclusion by distinguishing between earthly "solar years" and "divine years," herein described as Human Time and Divine Time.

Paleontology: the study of past life forms as represented in the fossil record.

Phylum: a group of organisms with a certain degree of morphological or developmental similarity. Morphology includes aspects of the outward appearance (shape, structure, color, and pattern) as well as the form and structure of the internal parts like bones and organs. In the biological classification hierarchy the phylum level has members numbering in the tens, whereas the more detailed species level has members numbering in the millions.

Pirkê De-Rabbi Eliezer ("Chapters of Rabbi Eliezer"): a Midrash that comprises ethical guidelines as well as astronomical discussions related to the Creation narrative.

Press/pulse model: a mass extinction model postulating that mass extinctions generally require two types of cause: long-term pressure on the eco-system ("press") and a sudden catastrophe ("pulse") toward the end of the pressure period.

Progressive creationists: a group that believes God intervened at various points in the geologic past to create the basic life forms that then evolved into the various species we know today.

Radioactive dating: measurement of the amount of radioactive material that an object contains; used to estimate the age of the object.

Radiometric dating: see Radioactive dating.

Ramban: Nahmanides, also known as Rabbi Moses ben Nachman Girondi, Bonastrucça Porta, and by his acronym Ramban (Gerona, 1194–Land of Israel, 1270); a leading medieval scholar, rabbi, philosopher, physician, Kabbalist, and biblical commentator.

Rank: see Taxonomy.

Rashi: Shlomo Yitzhaki (1040–1105 CE), better known by the acronym Rashi (RAbbi SHlomo Itzhaki); a medieval French rabbi famed as author of the first comprehensive commentary on the Talmud as well as a comprehensive commentary on the Written Law (including Genesis).

Science: the systematic process of gathering information about the world and organizing it into theories and laws that can be tested.

Scientific creationism: a branch of creationism that attempts to provide scientific support for the Genesis creation narrative in the Book of Genesis and disprove generally accepted scientific facts, theories, and scientific paradigms about the history of the earth, cosmology, and biological evolution.

Scientific method: a system of processes used to establish new or revised knowledge.

Sefirah (plural Sefirot): a channel of divine energy or life force. There are ten Sefirot. It is via the ten Sefirot that God interacts with creation; they may thus be considered His attributes.

Shmita: literally "release"; also called the Sabbatical Year; the seventh year of the seven-year agricultural cycle mandated by the Torah for the Land of Israel.

Sin: Adam's sin or primordial sin, wherein Adam ate the forbidden fruit of the Tree of Knowledge of Good and Bad. This sin occurred three hours before the end of Day 6.

Social Darwinism: a term that serves as a catch-all phrase to identify various utilitarian philosophies and policies that attribute human progress to unfettered competition among individuals.

Speciation: the evolutionary formation of new biological species, usually by the division of a single species into two or more genetically distinct ones.

Talmud: meaning instruction, learning; a central text of mainstream Judaism in the form of a record of rabbinic discussions pertaining to Jewish law, ethics, philosophy, customs and history.

Taxonomy: in biology, the science of classification in hierarchical structure. Each level in the hierarchical order is called rank. At the top of the hierarchy is life, followed by several levels of further subdivision, culminating with the lowest level, that of species.

Tetrapods: vertebrate animals having four limbs. They include amphibians, reptiles, birds, and mammals.

Theistic evolution: belief that accepts earthly species evolve but insists God has a role in the process.

Torah: consist of the Written Law and the Oral Law (see separate entry). The Written Law in turn consists of the Five Books of Moses, Prophets, Writings (or Psalms), Sanhedrin, Rabbinical Laws and Customs.

Trace fossils: marks left behind by an organism while it was alive, such as a footprint or feces.

Wisdom: considered the initial force in the creative process of the universe. It is the first Sefirah and corresponds to the element hydrogen.

Young earth creationism: form of creationism that asserts the universe and life were created by direct acts of God during a relatively short period, sometime between 5,700 and 10,000 years ago.

Zohar: meaning splendor, radiance; the foundational work in the literature of Jewish mystical thought known as Kabbalah.

Index

mass extinctions of life on earth, 131, 141
perspective on Adam, 148
timeline for appearance of land plants, 115
timeline for appearance of life, 121–123
timeline for development of the Universe, 97–98
Torah commentaries, 91–92
Torah Law, 172–173
trace fossils, 190
Tree of the Knowledge of Good and Bad, 136
Turkey, 27

Universe
age of, 1, 4–5, 85–88, 88n1
basic substance fashioned from, 93–94
expanding, 92–93
timeline for development of, 8–9, 35–38, 97–98

van Leeuwenhoek, Antonie, 110

Wallace, Alfred, 19
Western Europe, 27
Wilkinson Microwave Anisotropy Probe (WMAP), 86, 88n1
wisdom, 73, 190
WMAP. see Wilkinson Microwave Anisotropy Probe
Word of God, 5
Written Law, 14n4, 51

Yitzhaki, Shlomo, 59
young Earth creationism, 29n5, 190

Zabur, 6
Zohar, 7–8, 14n4, 57, 63–64, 161, 190

CPSIA information can be obtained at www.ICGtesting.com
Printed in the USA
LVOW06s1759070114

368463LV00007B/909/P